THIS IS...
citizenship

TERRY FIEHN
JULIA FIEHN

2

JOHN MURRAY

Key words are defined in the list on page 139.

First published 2002
by John Murray (Publishers) Ltd
50 Albemarle Street
London W1S 4BD

Layouts by Jenny Fleet
Artwork by Art Construction, Janek Matysiak, Tony Morris, Tony Randell, Chris Rothero/Linden Artists, Steve Smith
Typeset in 12/14pt Bodoni Book by Wearset Ltd, Boldon, Tyne and Wear
Colour separations by Colourscript, Mildenhall, Suffolk
Printed and bound in Spain by Bookprint, S. L., Barcelona

A catalogue entry for this book is available from the British Library.
ISBN 0 7195 7721 7
TRB 0 7195 7722 5

Contents

Acknowledgements

The authors and publishers would like to thank the following people and organisations for their help in the writing of this book:

- Louise Robinson, voluntary education consultant to the Fairtrade Foundation, now based at Reading International Solidarity Centre (RISC), for writing the material on fair trade in Section 6
- Nacro for providing information and advice on the writing of the materials in Section 1
- C-FAR and the young people involved in its rehabilitation scheme for supplying the information for the work on young offenders' institutions in Section 1.

Photographs and logos reproduced by kind permission of:
Cover Image State; **p.13** Barry Batchelor, Press Association Ltd; **p.21** European Press Agency, Press Association Ltd; **p.22** reproduction of Human Rights image with permission from the Lord Chancellor's Department; **p.28** *t* Disability Services, Queensland, Australia, *m and b* Commission for Racial Equality; **p.33** Phil Noble, The Press Association Ltd; **p.34** © Stockfile/Steven Behr; **p.35** *l* Phil Noble, The Press Association Ltd, *r* By permission Francesca Martinez; **p.54** *l* David Hoffman/Still Pictures, *r* David Hoffman/Still Pictures, *b* Environmental Images; **p.56** Helga Lade Fotoagentur; **p.64** *from top left* Copyright © The Labour Party, Copyright © Scottish Liberal Democrats, Copyright © Social Democrat and Labour Party, Copyright ©The Conservative Party, Copyright © Ulster Unionist Party, Copyright © Democratic Unionist Party, Copyright © Scottish Conservative and Unionist Party, Copyright © Scottish National Party, Help given by the Liberal Democrat Party, Copyright © Plaid Cymru, Copyright © Green Party of England and Wales, Copyright © UK Independence Party, © Copyright ProLife Alliance, With thanks to Alan Howling Lord Hope and Cat Mandu, Copyright © Third Way; **p.65** *tl* Kirsty Wigglesworth, The Press Association Ltd, *bl* Kevin Willocks, The Press Association Ltd, *br* Owen Humphreys, The Press Association Ltd; **p.68** *t* David Jones, The Press Association Ltd, *b* Dave Kendall, The Press Association Ltd; **p.72** *from top left* Copyright © Greenpeace, Copyright © Help the Aged, Copyright © Road Hauliers' Association, Copyright © National Union of Teachers, Copyright © Nacro, Copyright © Campaign for Nuclear Disarmament, Copyright © Amnesty International UK, Copyright © NSPCC, Copyright © RSPCA; **p.83** *bl* Copyright © Amnesty International UK, *br* © Carlos Retes-Manzo, Andes Press Agency; **p.88** Front page from © Times Newspapers Limited, 23 February 2002; **p.95** *t* Lesley Smith, Rex Features Ltd, *b* © Bubbles/Frans Rombout; **p.96** *t* Idols Picture Agency, *b* Kirsty Wigglesworth, The Press Association Ltd; **p.100** Peter Jordan, The Press Association Ltd; **p.101** Abaca Press, The Press Association Ltd; **pp.106–108** *all* © The Fairtrade Foundation; **p.110** *all* John Townson/Creation; **p.120** *l* Mike Shroder/Still Pictures, *m* © Axiom/Jim Holmes, *r* Nigel Dickinson/Still Pictures; **p.121** Janine Wiedel/David Hoffman Photo Library; **p.131** Adrian Baker, Photobank; **p.132** Christine Osborne Pictures; **p.133** © David Keith Jones, Images of Africa Photobank; **p.136** *t* Powerstock, *b* Ray Roberts/Rex Features.

t = top, *b* = bottom, *m* = middle, *r* = right, *l* = left

Text extracts reproduced by kind permission of:
pp.4–5 extracts from *Wasted Lives* © Nacro; **p.32** extracts from *Left Out, disabled people's access to goods and services* by Gwilym Morris and James Ford, published by Scope; **p.33** article from the *Sydney Morning Herald*, 2 May 2000; **p.96** article from *Metro*, 29 January 2002; **p.118** extract from *New Internationalist*, July 1997 (www.newint.org).

Every effort has been made to contact copyright holders, but if any have been inadvertently overlooked the publishers will be pleased to make the necessary arrangements at the earliest opportunity.

section 1

Rules, fairness and participation
Does the law treat young people fairly?

Key words
- court
- democracy
- justice
- law
- legal system
- magistrate
- offender
- police
- sentence

As children grow up, they learn about the rules of their family, friends, school and country. All groups of people need rules to protect the rights of each individual and of the group. Rules become laws when they are given the backing of the government of the country. Laws are written down and are enforced by the police. When people are accused of breaking the law, they are taken to court to try to find out if they are guilty or innocent. Courts can punish people found guilty of committing crimes.

Countries have different legal systems. Some have more laws than others; some have harsher punishments; some have fairer systems of dealing with people who are accused of breaking the law. In democratic countries, people can vote out a government if they don't like the laws it makes. In countries that are not democratic, it is more difficult for people to change things.

Laws are necessary, but there is always a balance to be struck between too many laws and too few. In this section we will look at how the law affects young people in the UK today. You will consider how fair or unfair the system is to young people who break the law and to the victims of their crimes.

In this section you will learn about:

* the law and young people
* the Criminal Justice System
* the work of the police
* the role of Youth Offending Teams
* Youth Courts.

You will:

* discover how the law affects young people
* discuss the law in small groups and in the whole class
* decide what you think is fair
* give your opinion and explain it to others
* think about other people's opinions and debate with them.

1.1 How does the law affect young people?

The law treats all adults the same. It is an important part of the legal system of the UK that the same laws apply to everyone. But the law allows young people to do different things at different ages. How much do you know about your legal rights and duties?

1 Work in pairs. At what age do you think you can do the following things? See how many you can get right. Your teacher will tell you the correct answers at the end.

13
Buy tobacco

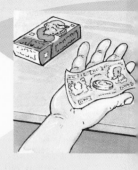

1
Be held to be criminally responsible

12
Marry with parent's consent

11
Give consent to heterosexual activity

2
Buy a pet

10
Fly an aeroplane

3
Get a part-time job

9
Buy fireworks

4
Go into a pub

8
Buy alcohol

7
Leave school

5
Get a custodial sentence for a crime

6
See a 15 certificate film

14
Join the
armed forces

2 Why are you allowed to do different things at different ages?
3 Which of these laws do you think are unfair?
4 Choose just one and plan an argument explaining why you
would like to see the law changed to a different age. Give
at least three reasons and explain them well.

26
Be entitled to
National Minimum Wage
(full adult rate)

15
Play the National
Lottery

25
Adopt a child

16
Drive
a car

24
Stand for
Parliament

23
Be entitled to
National Minimum Wage
(young person's
rate)

17
Have a
tattoo

22
Give consent to
homosexual
activity

18
Buy a
firearm

21
Buy a
house

19
Vote

20
Sign a
tenancy
agreement

1.2 Why do young people break the law?

No one of any age is allowed to break the law. Everyone over the age of ten can be arrested, tried and, if found guilty, punished. In England, Wales and Northern Ireland the law says that children under the age of ten are not 'criminally responsible'. (In Scotland, the age is eight.) This means that children younger than this probably do not understand that what they have done is wrong. If a child under the age of criminal responsibility does commit a serious crime, social services will deal with the case.

Activity

Read these extracts (A–G) below. What do they tell you about the reasons why some young people get into trouble?

These extracts come from the book *Wasted lives* published by the National Association for the Care and Resettlement of Offenders (Nacro)

A 'At the end of the day I still think it was me, right, just going all mad. But little things just push you in one direction or just help you along your way ... '

B ' It's all about who they grew up with and what they know ... If you grew up in a good area with all kids that are good and that, there's [not much chance] that they're gonna do crime, but when you grew up in a rough area, with all people doing crime, smoking dope and whatever, doing drugs, the kids that grew up in that area they've got a bigger chance that he'll end up like that as well.'

C 'I had people say to me, yeah it's your fault you're in jail, but it ain't my fault. I'm the one that's been slung out of my house at eleven years of age, no mum to love me, no brothers, nothing. I had to go out into the big wide world to fight for myself, find food for myself, find clothes and all this ... It is the mother's and father's fault ... It's the love that your family has to give you, that can stop [offending], nothing else. If your mum and dad shows you neglect I guarantee you you're going into crime.'

D 'I call him dad 'cause he's been with me since I was two ... me mum's not with him any more 'cause he started beating her up and beating me and me brother Keith up ... He used to beat us with them [carpet rods] ... I've grown up with violence all around.'

E 'On the street you're looking for a hard reputation ... When you're younger you just look up at older people and you say yeah man look at them rings he's got on, I want them rings man ... go out and get the money go buy the rings, that's the way it goes.'

F 'Kids hang out in groups, some of them are criminals already, get new friends and they dare them to do a house robbery or something like that ... so they end up going to do it and they get lucky and get away with it ... so they can make easy money instead of going out working ... if you think about it they can earn about £1000 in no time by doing a house or two ... not a likely chance of getting caught, so why not?'

G 'Problems at home led me to hang around street corners as it were. I got into drugs, I didn't have any money so I started stealing, then I got on to harder, you know higher up the scale like car theft, things like that.'

Discuss

1 Look at the list of reasons (right) that have been suggested as to why young people break the law. Discuss them in a small group and decide whether you think each one is a significant reason. Are there any other reasons you think should be listed, or would you remove any?

2 Try to decide which are the six reasons that you think would be most likely to lead young people towards crime.

3 Discuss these in class to see if everybody agrees.

4 What would you guess are the three most common crimes committed by young people under the age of eighteen?

* Work in pairs and discuss this for a few minutes. Decide on your top three.
* See how much agreement there is in the class. Discuss why there is or is not agreement.
* Do you think that television and newspapers influence your ideas about what crimes are being committed?
* Do you have personal experience of these crimes?

Reasons why young people break the law

* Not getting on well at school
* Parents unable to control them
* Influenced by friends
* Not very intelligent
* Come from a poor family
* Bored and looking for fun
* Trying to impress other young people
* Looking for adult attention
* Feeling as if they are not respected
* Unhappy
* History of crime in the family
* No respect for other people
* Drugs/alcohol
* Parents split up
* Harsh discipline
* No skills
* Feeling unloved

5 Invite a police officer or a member of the local Youth Offending Team (YOT) to come into school. Interview him or her about the reasons why young people commit crimes and which crimes are the commonest.

1.3 What happens to young offenders when they are caught?

If a young person (aged ten to seventeen) commits a first, minor offence, they might get a *reprimand* (an official telling-off). If they offend again, they will be given a *final warning*. This means they will be referred to a Youth Offending Team who will try to help the young person stay out of trouble.

If the young person offends again, or if the first offence is serious, they will be sent straight to a Youth Court for trial and, if convicted, sentence.

Activity

What do you think should happen to each of these offenders (right)? Should they:

* get a reprimand
* receive a final warning and go to the Youth Offending Team
* be sent to the Youth Court?

Think about how old each offender is, what they have done and how serious the offence is.

First offence (probably not too serious) – informal warning or reprimand if the young person admits guilt.

Police
The decision by the police to give a reprimand or a final warning depends on:

* the seriousness of the offence
* whether the young person has been in trouble before.

So, if the offence is not too serious, and the young person has not been in trouble with the police before and admits their guilt, usually they will be given a reprimand. They cannot receive a second reprimand.

If the offence is serious, then the young person will be charged and go straight to the Youth Court.

Second offence – final warning and referral to Youth Offending Team.

Youth Offending Team
The YOT is made up of members of the police and social services, and education, probation and health agencies in a local area. The team decides what action needs to be taken to stop the young person from offending again.

If the offender is under ten, there will be no trial, but the Youth Court will be asked to make a Child Safety Order (see page 16).

Next offence (or first serious offence) – charged by the police and prosecuted in a Youth Court.

Youth Court
This is a special court for young people, heard by magistrates. The magistrates decide whether the young person is guilty, and, if so, what the punishment should be.

Mohamed is nine years old and has been getting into trouble a lot at school. He was seen on camera smashing cars in the school car park. This is not his first case of vandalism. He is well-known on his estate for breaking windows and getting into fights. Teachers at the school are worried that he will get hurt himself, as well as causing damage to property.

Janice is fifteen and a mother of a small boy aged six months. She was caught shoplifting from a clothes store. It is her first offence. She says she has no money to buy clothes and wanted something for a party. She is a good mother and is very worried that the baby will be put into care if she is taken into custody.

Michael is thirteen and has been arrested for burglary of a shop. He has not been in trouble before and his role in this offence was fairly minor – he was the look-out. The other three involved were older boys who persuaded him to go along. His mother is very upset and has grounded him. He has been misbehaving at school recently. He says he is sorry and promises not to get into trouble again.

Trevor is sixteen and has stolen an elderly woman's handbag in the street. He used no weapon, but pushed her to the ground. He already has a final warning from the police for theft. His parents are not able to control Trevor and have been unhelpful to the Youth Offending Team during the last few months. They say he has got in with a bad lot of friends.

Stevie is sixteen. He has been arrested for taking a vehicle and driving it away with a group of friends. They had all been drinking heavily. Stevie was driving the car and got involved in a car chase with the police. The car eventually crashed into a wall. Luckily no one was seriously hurt, but the car was a write-off. This is his first offence and he says he is sorry.

Marcia is fourteen and has been found in possession of drugs – mostly pills. The police suspect that she has been supplying them to other young people. They have also seen her out late at night in the red-light area of the city, and think that she might be involved in prostitution. She lives with her mother, who works a night shift and denies that Marcia might be in this kind of trouble.

The Youth Offending Team

If a young person gets a final warning, they are referred to a Youth Offending Team (YOT). Usually one member of the team will take responsibility for the young person, although two or three other members of the team may also be involved, e.g. an education specialist and a health worker. The people on the YOT will draw up a programme for the young person and their family. The programme will try to change the young person's attitudes and behaviour. For example, the young person may be asked to go along to group sessions on anger management.

The programme might cover things like:

* reasons why the young person got into trouble
* help for parents to control the young person better
* counselling for the young person
* community activities
* an apology to the victim and repair of any damage
* improving school work and attendance.

The programme is not a punishment. It is meant to stop the young person reoffending. However, if within two years of the programme the young person commits another offence and goes to court, they will not be able to get a conditional discharge (be allowed off on condition that no further offence is committed).

On the right is a made-up programme for a young person who has been caught causing criminal damage by spraying graffiti on walls whilst truanting from school.

PROGRAMME FOR JOHN HARRINGE

■ Attend school on a regular basis and keep a record card showing attendance, to be signed by the headteacher.

■ Attend three sessions with a YOT worker looking at the consequences of his actions.

■ Assist a local community group that is preparing a mural in a local youth club.

Activity

Remember Michael?

Michael is thirteen and has been arrested for burglary of a shop. He has not been in trouble before and his role in this offence was fairly minor – he was the look-out. The other three involved were older boys who persuaded him to go along. His mother is very upset and has grounded him. He has been misbehaving at school recently. He says he is sorry and promises not to get into trouble again.

Imagine you are a member of a Youth Offending Team working with Michael, one of the young offenders on page 7.

Some teams are very large with over 50 members of staff; others will have around ten members. Usually five or six will work with a particular offender. You will work with about six other pupils. Decide what role each member of the team is going to take. The team might be made up of:

* police officers
* social workers
* a teacher
* a magistrate

* a drugs worker
* a mental health nurse
* a probation officer
* a youth worker.

Try to act as your character might. A police officer, for example, might have a different attitude to that of a social worker. You have to draw up a programme for Michael. Decide what is likely to help Michael to stop offending and have a more successful life.

REPORT

Michael's father recently left the family after rows with Michael's mother. Michael hasn't seen his father for a few months. Michael has become friendly with a group of older boys who have left school or dropped out early. He met them at the youth club. All of the older boys have been in trouble with the police. Michael hasn't been seeing many of his previous friends recently and has stopped going to the chemistry club that his friends still go to after school on Wednesdays.

Michael's teachers think he could do well in his exams if he worked a bit harder. Until the trouble at home, he had been getting good marks, particularly in science. Michael has said he would like a career in forensic science, but he has lost confidence in his own ability. He now says he doesn't expect to achieve this.

The Youth Court

If young people commit a serious offence, or if they reoffend after a final warning, the case goes to a Youth Court. The Youth Court is a type of magistrates' court specially designed for young people under the age of eighteen. It is less formal than adult courts, the magistrates are specially trained and they have a different range of sentences they can pass. The cases are held in private: members of the public are not allowed in. The parents of the young person are generally expected to attend.

Magistrates
Two or three magistrates sit behind a big desk (the bench). They are men and women chosen from the community (not lawyers) who decide whether the young person has committed the offence and how they are going to be dealt with. Most magistrates are not paid. One of the magistrates (usually the one in the middle) is the chairperson and speaks for them all.

Witness
A police officer might give details of the offence or another person might say what happened. Witnesses only attend if the young person says he or she is not guilty.

Usher
The usher calls in the witnesses and keeps out members of the public who are not allowed to be present.

Youth Offending Team (see page 8)
Some of the team might attend. They sit at the back of the court.

Young person, parents and solicitor
The young person who is charged with the offence (the defendant) sits in the middle of the court in front of the bench. The parents sit on one side and a solicitor usually sits on the other. The solicitor is a trained lawyer who knows the law and is there to protect the legal rights of the young person.

Justice's clerk
The clerk sits at the side or in front of the magistrates. The clerk is a trained lawyer and advises the magistrates on the law. They are responsible for the day-to-day running of the court. The clerk reads out the charge (the offence the young person is said to have committed) and asks whether he/she pleads guilty or not. The clerk has no say in deciding whether the young person is guilty and does not decide what should happen to them, although he/she may tell the magistrates what alternatives (see right) are open to them.

Prosecutor
The prosecutor is a solicitor whose job is to set out the case against the young person for the police. They provide the evidence to show that the person committed the offence.

Victim
Victims may come to court if they wish, and may be involved before the magistrates decide on any sentence.

The Youth Court can make a number of 'orders' if the young person is found guilty.

* **reparation order** – The young offender is told by the court to repair whatever they have damaged in committing the crime or to carry out other work of benefit to the community. This could involve repairing damage, writing an apology, or meeting the victim face to face to talk about the crime. The Youth Offending Team makes sure this happens.

* **action plan order** – The Youth Offending Team draws up a three-month sentence of community work for the young offender. This order can require offenders to:
  – take part in activities such as anger-management classes or drug/alcohol misuse programmes
  – present themselves at particular times at specified places
  – go to an attendance centre for a certain number of hours
  – stay away from specified places, e.g. shopping centres
  – follow certain educational arrangements
  – make reparation to identified persons (for example, apologise) or the community (for example, clean a local canal)
  – attend a court review within 21 days.

* **custodial detention and training order** – The court may sentence a young person over twelve to a period of time in custody. Half of the sentence is spent in either a local authority secure unit or a secure training centre. The other half of the sentence is spent under supervision in the community. Offenders over fifteen can be sent to a young offenders' institution.

Parenting order

In addition to the other orders, the court can also hand out a parenting order. The parents are told by the court to have greater control over their child. The parents may have to attend parenting classes to learn how to do this. A fine of £1000 is made if the parents do not agree to do this.

Activity

Remember Trevor?

Trevor is sixteen and has stolen an elderly woman's handbag in the street. He used no weapon, but pushed her to the ground. He already has a final warning from the police for theft. His parents are not able to control Trevor and have been unhelpful to the Youth Offending Team during the last few months. They say he has got in with a bad lot of friends.

Either:

1 Work in groups of two or three. Imagine you are the magistrates in a Youth Court. Trevor has come before you. Read the report below and then decide which of the orders you will make on Trevor.

Or:

2 The class divides into two or three groups. Members of each group take on the roles of the three magistrates, the clerk, Trevor's solicitor, the prosecutor, a police officer, Trevor and Trevor's parents.

   Act out the Youth Court procedure (see the box on the right). Then present it to the rest of the class. You can add extra details about what happened, witnesses, etc.

3 Invent some cases for yourself and take them through the Youth Court. For instance, one could involve taking and driving away a car which results in somebody getting injured. Discuss the impact of a crime on the victim (e.g. an elderly woman or a young boy who has been beaten up). Also think about what can be done to make offenders realise what they have done and be sorry about it.

Youth Court procedure

1 The clerk reads out the charges and checks that the young person understands what the charges mean.
2 The young person (defendant) pleads 'guilty' or 'not guilty'.
3 If the defendant pleads 'guilty', sentencing takes place.
4 If the defendant pleads 'not guilty', the case proceeds.
5 Witnesses are called and the police give evidence. The prosecutor sets out the case against the defendant and calls witnesses for the prosecution. The defence can call witnesses to support its case.
6 After all the evidence has been heard, the magistrates decide whether the defendant is guilty or not.
7 If the defendant is found guilty, the magistrates pass sentence (one or more of the orders shown on page 11).
8 The magistrates can ask the Youth Offending Team to prepare a report on the offender if they do not feel they have enough information to pass sentence. If the offender is likely to get a custodial sentence (locked up in a secure unit or young offenders' institution) they may request a pre-sentence report.

REPORT

As magistrates, you have already received a report on Trevor from the Youth Offending Team. You also now know that he is out of control at home. His parents say he often stays out all night and they don't know where he is. They think he may be involved with a gang of young people who take a variety of drugs. He often truants from school, and his teachers say that he will not be entered for many exams because of his poor attendance.

Trevor and his friends are feared by the people on his estate. There is no proof, but the police think he is part of a group of boys who steal other residents' cars and joy-ride. Trevor was given a programme by the Youth Offending Team six months earlier when he was caught stealing a radio from a car on the estate. He has not kept his side of the contract on the programme and has failed to keep appointments with social workers and his mentor (an older person who offers support and advice). He has not said he is sorry for the offence and has been rude and abusive to everyone involved.

1.4 Inside a young offenders' institution

If a young offender is over the age of fifteen, he or she can be sentenced to custody in a young offenders' institution (YOI). What is it like inside? What experiences do the young people have? Does it help them or does it turn them into hardened criminals?

The views below are compiled from interviews with several young people who have spent quite a lot of time in YOIs. Most of them have long records of offending stretching back to the ages of twelve and thirteen. What they have in common now is the desire not to spend any more time in prison.

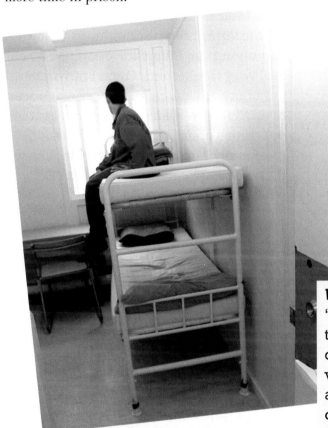

What are YOIs like inside?

'The YOIs in old prisons can be dirty, paint peeling off walls and the like. Others are modern or have been done up and are all right. The cells are small and usually you share. Apart from a double bunk bed you have a table, a washbasin and metal chairs fixed to the wall – not much else. You can have a radio and a CD player. But whatever the cells are like it does your head in to be stuck in them for so long each day. The boredom is a real killer.'

What's the daily routine like?

'It varies with the institution. In some of them you're banged up in your cell for over eighteen hours a day and you get very little exercise and not much association time – that's mixing with other inmates. In other places you're banged up for less time, fifteen to sixteen hours. You get more leisure time, say, two hours' association time every evening, one hour's exercise, two hours' education, and so on. But you often spend a lot of time in your cell. In some places you can get jobs and earn some money (not much) gardening, in the kitchens, or as a landing cleaner. You can spend that on your canteen. Once a week you are given your money, about £2.50, and you can spend it on tobacco, sweets, that kind of thing.'

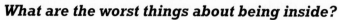

What are the worst things about being inside?

'You don't know what's going on outside. Say you've got trouble with your family. It only takes one person to say something and, together with everything else that's in your head, it makes you feel bad and frustrated because you can't do anything. Also with girlfriends there's so much stress; you think she's out clubbing; she's seeing someone; you feel paranoid because you don't know what's going on – it drives you mad … And there's never enough food! You're always hungry… And the boredom!

There's a lot of violence and bullying. In prison you've got nothing, so things mean something. I've seen a fight over a packet of biscuits. Whenever somebody has something others think they should have a share. And there'll always be someone who takes it all to show how hard they are. If you go round the cells in a prison, there will always be people who can't fight to save their lives. But they can survive in jail by bartering: swap something; sell something; do things for people. You can feel very threatened. Once I never came out of my cell much for two weeks because five lads were waiting to get me. I sat in my cell with a chair leg ready to have a go. Eventually I got myself put into solitary and then got shipped out to another YOI.'

Do YOIs help you to change?

'In some ways they make things worse because you build up a network of new contacts with criminals, people who say 'See me when you get out,' and they introduce you to their friends and get you drugs, etc. Also you feel so angry and frustrated that when you do get out you're likely to go and get yourself into trouble.

The education – basic maths and English, cooking, computers – is quite useful. But the officers, apart from a few, aren't interested much. You can't blame them, they're just doing a job, and most of the inmates don't want help, they just want to do their time and get out and go back to their old life. In three and a half years only one officer, a female officer, has been really helpful and tried to encourage me to change when I leave prison. You need much more advice about how to get jobs and more help to find places to live and start again in a new place. Because if you go back to where you were you just slip into your old ways.'

Activity

All YOIs are inspected regularly. The inspectors make recommendations about improvements that could be made. Some of the things they look at are:

* Prisoners' everyday lives (e.g. accommodation, visits, education)
* Custody and control (e.g. bullying, security, use of restraint)
* Care and resettlement (e.g. first night, community activities, transfer, release)
* Management and staffing
* The building and facilities.

Choose two of these headings and say what recommendations you would make to improve young offenders' institutions from the information that you have read on these two pages.

1.5 The youth justice system

Restorative justice

Much of the youth justice system is based on the idea of restorative justice. The three main objectives of this are:

* Responsibility – young people taking responsibility for their behaviour and offences and being encouraged to behave more responsibly in the future
* Restoration – young people making amends to their victims or to the community in general
* Reintegration – providing guidance and support to get offenders back into society and helping them to develop as law-abiding citizens.

Main features of youth justice

The present system was set up by the Crime and Disorder Act 1998 and the Youth Justice and Criminal Evidence Act 1999. The main aim is to 'prevent offending by young people' using the ideas of restorative justice (see above).

Two new bodies were created:

1 The Youth Justice Board (YJB) monitors the work of Youth Offending Teams and of the youth justice system, advises the Home Secretary and promotes good practice.
2 Youth Offending Teams (YOTs) – made up of social workers, police officers, probation officers and health and education workers:

* support police reprimands and warnings
* supervise community sentences
* prepare reports for courts and do court work
* are involved in the care of young people throughout and after custodial sentences.

The process of youth justice

1 If a young person between the ages of ten and seventeen is believed to have committed a criminal offence, the police can give the offender an 'informal warning' or 'telling-off'. This does not count as a criminal record and is used for first or minor offences.

2 The police can issue a reprimand or a final warning if the young person has admitted guilt. These are given at a police station, and if the young person is under seventeen, in the presence of an appropriate adult.
3 A final warning results in the young person being referred to a Youth Offending Team (YOT). The YOT will arrange a programme to 'rehabilitate' the offender. This may involve reparation (apology, financial compensation, donation to charity, community activity), counselling, education and skills development, parenting skills and mentoring (see page 11).
4 If the young person does not carry out the final warning programme, if the offence is more serious, or if the young person reoffends, he/she will be sent to the Youth Court (see pages 10–11). The Youth Court is not open to the public. The court procedure is described on page 12.
5 Magistrates can impose the following sentences:

* a fine
* compensation order (money paid to victim)
* parents 'bound over' to exercise control over offender and make sure that any community orders are followed. They forfeit £1000 if the young person offends again.
* reparation order (see page 11)
* parenting order (see page 11)
* action plan order (see page 11)
* attendance centre – go to centre, usually run by police, for two hours twice a month for between twelve and thirty-six hours
* curfew order – offender has to remain in a particular place at certain specified times, e.g. at home after 9p.m.
* supervision order – offender supervised by social worker, probation officer or another member of a YOT for between three months and three years
* community rehabilitation order
* custodial sentence – young person is locked up in a secure unit or a young offenders' institution.

* child safety order – child is supervised by a member of the YOT to make sure that he/she has appropriate support and to prevent them becoming involved again in crime or anti-social behaviour. The supervising officer may devise a programme of activities for them.

The table below shows the ages at which you can legally do or be held responsible for certain activities.

Activity	Age
1 Be held to be criminally responsible	10 (8 in Scotland)
2 Buy a pet	12
3 Get a part-time job	13
4 Go into a pub	14
5 Get a custodial sentence for a crime	15
6 See a 15 certificate film	15
7 Leave school	16
8 Buy alcohol	18
9 Buy fireworks	18
10 Fly an aeroplane	16
11 Give consent to heterosexual activity	16
12 Marry with parent's consent	16 (without consent in Scotland)
13 Buy tobacco	16
14 Join the armed forces	16 (with parent's consent)
15 Play the National Lottery	16
16 Drive a car	17
17 Have a tattoo	18
18 Buy a firearm	17
19 Vote	18
20 Sign a tenancy agreement	18 (16 in Scotland)
21 Buy a house	18
22 Give consent to homosexual activity	18
23 Be entitled to National Minimum Wage (young person's rate)	18
24 Stand for Parliament	21
25 Adopt a child	21
26 Be entitled to the National Minimum Wage (full adult rate)	22

section 2

Human rights and responsibilities
Equal rights for all?

Key words
- civil liberties
- discrimination
- election
- equal opportunities
- human rights
- motion

People in the UK expect their rights to be protected. There is a long history of people fighting for different rights such as the right to vote, the right to own property and the right to express an opinion. In some countries in the world today, people have few rights, and they can be imprisoned without a reason, tortured, forced into slavery, even killed.

After the Second World War the countries of Europe signed up to the European Convention for the Protection of Human Rights. The UK has a Human Rights Act, which says that the Convention is also part of our law. The Human Rights Act 2000 covers a lot of different rights, including the right to life, the right to marry and have a family, and the right to own property.

The vast majority of people would agree that basic human rights such as freedom from torture or freedom of speech should be observed. But there are some areas where it is not so easy to decide about the rights people should have.

People believe that they live in a free society and have the 'right' to behave as they wish. This may bring them into conflict with other people, who feel that such behaviour affects their 'rights'. For example, a group of young people might feel that they have the right to play loud music whenever they want while their neighbours might feel they have the right to a good night's sleep. To sort these problems out, people have to behave responsibly towards each other, although this does not mean that they have to agree.

In this section you will learn about:

* rights and responsibilities
* how the law protects rights
* conflicting rights
* the rights of some minority groups, for example, people with disabilities.

You will:

* make decisions about moral and social issues
* analyse information about rights and responsibilities
* give your opinion and justify it
* take part in group discussion and debates
* use your imagination to consider how other people might feel in different situations.

2.1 Right or wrong?

People sometimes do not recognise that their behaviour affects other people's rights. For example, smoking in public or having fun at a loud party could affect the rights of someone else. We need to think about how to balance one person's rights against another person's. The law tries to protect everyone's rights, but sometimes there is disagreement.

1 In pairs, look at the following situations. Decide whether you agree with each person.

2 When you have decided which people you agree with, join up with another pair and see if you all feel the same way.

3 Choose two situations where you think the person has a good case and decide what should happen. Your teacher can tell you the legal position in each situation.

Fred Jones and his wife have twin toddlers. They love to take the twins out on Saturdays to eat in a restaurant in the town centre. They believe they have a right to take the children wherever they go. Sometimes the twins argue and fight, run about and make a terrible noise in the restaurant. Other customers complain that they have the right to a peaceful meal.

Jo Cheung is a keen supporter of animal rights. She intends to demonstrate in a big rally that has been planned outside a research laboratory. The police have decided to cancel the rally because of the likely danger to workers at the laboratory. Jo says her rights to make her views known have been denied by the police.

Mehmet Ali likes to smoke a cigarette between each course when he eats. It helps his enjoyment of the meal. Sometimes when he visits his local restaurant, all the smoking tables are taken and he has to sit in the non-smoking section of the restaurant. He thinks he should be able to have a cigarette when he wants one, but people at nearby tables complain about the smoke.

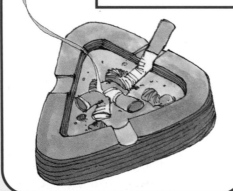

Jane Simpson has written a magazine article about people who come from a particular country. It is a very critical article and says some very unpleasant things. The editor of the magazine says he will not publish the article because it would offend people. Jane argues that she has a right to freedom of expression, to say what she believes to be the truth.

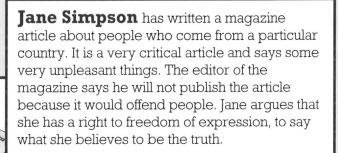

Mary Brown is worried that a mobile phone mast is about to be erected on the building next door. She thinks it will be a hazard to the health of her children and says that her right to a healthy environment will be affected. However, the phone company says that there must be more masts if mobile phone users are to be able to use their phones.

Harry Tanner has a large, noisy dog. It barks all the time, night and day. Harry says it keeps burglars away and he loves it very much. It is his companion. The neighbours can take no more of the barking and are demanding that he either moves or gets rid of the dog. Harry says he has a right to keep it.

Maroula Mitchell has found out that her employer has been monitoring her e-mails to her boyfriend from the company computer. The employer says she is wasting time at work, but Maroula says she has a right to privacy and to communicate with friends if she wishes.

2.2 A woman's right to choose?

Wendy Harrington is ten weeks pregnant. She does not wish to have the child, since she is only seventeen years old and does not want a long-term relationship with the father. She has decided to have an abortion and believes it is a woman's right to choose. However, the father of the child wants her to have the baby and says he will care for it. He feels he has the right to demand that the child be born. Wendy's aunt is religious and is a member of a pro-life group which believes that every foetus has a right to life.

This is a serious debate about rights in conflict. What arguments would the three put forward?

1 Look at the points below and decide who would use each one. One point for each side has been done for you.

Wendy	The father	The aunt (pro-life)
A woman has the right to decide what happens to her own body.	A person shouldn't be denied the right to bring up his own child.	Every person has the right to life and a foetus is a person.

A foetus is not a person; it is a bundle of cells without feelings or consciousness.

A woman who does not choose to become pregnant should be able to end the pregnancy.

God gives life; it is not up to human beings to decide who lives and dies.

A child can ruin a young woman's career before it has even begun and will determine the rest of her life.

A foetus is carrying both parents' genes, so it is part of the father as much as the mother.

A father who is prepared to look after the child should have a say.

Fathers are supposed to take responsibility for babies, so they have a right to say what happens to the foetus.

It's the woman who has to carry and bear the child and look after it.

It is morally wrong and wicked to kill the foetus.

It is irresponsible to run the risk of getting pregnant when you don't want to have a baby – people should not have sex or they should take proper precautions.

It is not a good idea to bring an unwanted child into the world.

Debate

2 You have now sorted out some of the main points for and against abortion in this case, although the points are not fully explained.

  a) The class should split into three groups. Each group adopts one of the positions.

  b) Each group should develop the arguments for this position, adding any others they can think of.

  c) Hold a debate. Two people from each group should make the opening statements in the debate. Then everybody else can join in. The rules of debate can be found on Info page 38.

Discuss

3 After the debate, decide which argument you agree with most. Do other people agree? Has anyone's opinion been changed?

4 Think back over the debate and the situations you looked at on pages 18–19.

  a) Why is the issue of rights a difficult one?

  b) Is it always easy to decide whose rights are the most important in a situation?

  c) Do you think there will always be conflicts of rights? Why?

'My Body My Choice': Pro-choice campaigners believe that a woman has a right to choose what happens in her own body. They campaign against laws restricting abortions.

'Abortion Kills Children': Pro-life campaigners believe it is always wrong to abort a foetus. They try to persuade women not to have abortions and politicians to make laws against abortion.

2.3 The Human Rights Act

Until October 2000, if people in the UK believed that their human rights had been denied, they could take their case to the European Court of Human Rights. Here, European judges decided whether what had happened to them was against the European Convention for the Protection of Human Rights (ECHR). Now the ECHR has been made part of British law under the Human Rights Act 1998, and people don't have to go to Europe to bring a case. The Human Rights Act 1998 came into full force from 2 October 2000.

The rights apply to everyone in the UK, whether or not they are British citizens, and the government must make sure they receive their rights. You can find out more about the Articles of the ECHR on Info page 36.

Activity

Look at each of the cases opposite and answer these questions.

1 What problems do these people face?
2 Which rights have been denied them?
3 What do you think should happen in each case to resolve the problem?

The Human Rights Act covers the following areas:

- ☆ Everyone has the right to life.
- ☆ No one can be tortured or given degrading punishment.
- ☆ No one can be held in slavery or forced labour.
- ☆ Everyone has the right to liberty and security.
- ☆ Anyone accused of a crime is entitled to a fair and public hearing in court.
- ☆ No one can be punished for an action which was not a crime when it was committed.
- ☆ Everyone has the right to privacy and family life.
- ☆ Everyone has the right to freedom of opinions and religion.
- ☆ Everyone has the right to freedom of expression.
- ☆ Everyone has the right to protest peacefully and to join, or not to join, a trade union.
- ☆ Men and women of marriageable age have the right to marry and have a family.
- ☆ Everyone had the right to own and enjoy their property.
- ☆ No one can be denied the right to an education.
- ☆ There must be free elections at regular intervals, with secret voting, so that people can choose their own government.
- ☆ The death penalty is abolished.
- ☆ No one can be discriminated against, on any grounds, in getting these rights.

HUMAN RIGHTS
comes to life

Case 1

A thirteen-year-old boy has been disruptive at his school ever since he arrived there at the beginning of Year 7. The parents of other pupils in the class have complained that he is preventing their children from making educational progress. The headteacher of the school has decided that the boy is to be excluded permanently from the school. No other school in the area is prepared to take him because of his record of misbehaviour, which includes violence towards teachers. His mother says she is going to take up the matter under the Human Rights Act.

Case 2

A council has announced that it is building a waste tip next to houses on the outskirts of a town. The people who live in the houses believe that the waste tip will be a major health risk, especially for their children. It is likely to give off gases and might pollute the local water supply. They have declared that they are going to take the council to court under the Human Rights Act.

Case 3

A 53-year-old man is suffering from heart disease. He has already had one heart by-pass operation, but his condition has become serious again and he needs another operation. However, his doctors say that he has continued smoking and eating unhealthy foods, so that he is now more overweight than he was originally. They will not treat him unless he is prepared to take some action to improve his own health; otherwise, the operation would be a waste of time. The man, who is in danger of dying, says he will take the hospital to court under the Human Rights Act.

Case 4

A young doctor has arrived from Iraq seeking asylum. In Iraq he was imprisoned, badly beaten and had half his index finger cut off because his torturers thought he had information to give them. His father paid a gang to get him to Britain. He spent twelve days in a lorry container before he arrived. In Britain, he has been given accommodation and money to buy food. He is desperate to work, but no one will give him a job. People have sworn at him in the street and some youths punched and kicked him. He now stays indoors most of the time because he is frightened to go out on to the streets. He feels like he is back in prison.

2.4 We know where you are!

It is now possible to track ordinary people as they go about their everyday lives. New technology is making it easier all the time for the authorities to pinpoint where people are and what they are doing at any time. Many towns and cities have closed circuit television (CCTV) cameras for security purposes. So do shops, stations and retail parks. Cameras on motorways record which cars are speeding where and how fast. We can also be located when we use machines to take out cash, and when we use credit or debit cards to pay for petrol, train tickets, and goods in shops. Calls from mobile phones and e-mails can also be traced to a particular spot.

Mobile phone
Sophisticated devices can listen in to conversations. Even when the phone is on stand-by, it is in contact with the base station, telling it where you are.

Credit Card
Paying by credit card shows where you have been, and a record of what you buy.

CCTV
In many shops, public places and even streets, closed circuit television cameras film and record people as they go about their daily lives.

Activity

Look at the trail left by Sam, who went on a journey across the country one day. Can you work out where she was and when?

Use a chart like this one below to help you. The first entry has been done for you.

Time	Place	Evidence
8.30a.m.	Brighton	bank withdrawal slip

WHEELS-R-US
Car and van Rental

Rental Agreement   Brighton   Office

VEHICLE DETAILS		CUSTOMER
Reg Number Y564DFS		Ms Sam Brown
Model Almera		42 Hove Road
Branch from Brighton		Brighton
Branch to Peterborough		

	DATE	TIME	LICENCE NO
OUT	15/03/2002	09:02	BROWN12345ABSS
IN	16/03/2002	13:00	

CHARGES £35.00
VAT   £6.13
PAYMENT   £41.13

METHOD OF PAYMENT
VISA
4876543212 3456789

Signed Sam Brown.   Date 15/03/02

County Bank
AT BRIGHTON
08:30 15MAR02

WITHDRAWAL

£100.00

REF GN71509

THANK YOU

WHEELS-R-US

From security camera G783 at
09:00: 16-03-02

Car
As you travel, you may be filmed by CCTV and your numberplate recorded by automated camera systems.

E-mail and internet
Billions of e-mails are thought to be intercepted every day, for security checks. If you receive just one message from a known or suspected criminal or terrorist, you can be suspected, too.
And computers keep a record of internet activity.

We all like to think the UK is a 'free country' where we can come and go as we please. People do not expect to be tracked, unless they have committed a crime.

Sam has rights, sometimes called 'civil liberties', which means that she ought to be free from unnecessary surveillance by anyone. However, someone has to decide when surveillance is necessary and when it is not.

Activity

Work in a small group and look at the cases on the right.

1 **Think about whether Sam should be tracked down in each of them. Give your reasons in each case.**

2 **Choose one of the cases where you think Sam should *not* be tracked down. Say why you think her right to privacy should be protected in this case.**

Discuss

Is increased surveillance in the UK a good or a bad thing?

1 **When can it be helpful?**

2 **When could individuals or governments put it to unpleasant or dangerous uses?**

A Sam has forgotten to take some medicine with her on the trip and her son is frantically worried that she will become ill.

B Sam is suspected of belonging to a terrorist organisation that may be planning to explode a bomb in York.

C Sam's boss suspects she is sending in fiddled expense claims and wants to know how far she really did travel.

D Sam is very critical of the government and belongs to a group of anarchists who are planning a peaceful demonstration at a conference in the north of the country.

E Sam's mother has been involved in a serious accident and has been rushed to hospital in Brighton.

F A robbery took place at a shop in Cambridge at about 1.45p.m. Sam's car shows up on a CCTV camera in the area near the time of the robbery. All suspects are being checked by the police.

G Sam's husband suspects she is having an affair with a man in York and is having her movements tracked by a private detective.

H Sam is a spy and is passing on secrets to an agent from another country.

2.5 Equal opportunities for all?

In the UK there are other laws that protect people's rights, as well as the Human Rights Act. It is against the law to discriminate against someone because of their race or their sex, and there is also some protection from discrimination for people with disabilities. Discrimination can happen in lots of different areas of life: housing, benefits, schools, hospitals, and particularly at work.

Activity

The laws shown in the panel on the right make it illegal to discriminate against people directly or indirectly or, in the case of disabled people, to treat them 'less favourably' than non-disabled people.

In which of the following examples of people applying for jobs has the law been broken? You can get some extra help from Info pages 37–38.

- A job in a bank requires female workers to wear a skirt, but one applicant wears trousers for religious reasons and therefore does not get the job.

- A job at a call centre is advertised. Applicants must have 'clear spoken English'.

- A single mother wants a live-in nanny, and advertises for a 'young woman'.

- An applicant does not get a job because she would not be able to do shift work as she has children.

- Someone does not get an office job because he is a wheelchair user. There are stairs at the offices and no lift.

- A worker does not get a job on a building site because it involves wearing a safety helmet and, as a Sikh, he wears a turban.

Discrimination and the law

* The Sex Discrimination Act 1975 makes it illegal to discriminate against someone because of their sex.

* The Race Relations Act 1976 (amended 2000) makes it illegal to discriminate against someone because of colour, race, nationality or ethnic origin.

Both *direct* and *indirect* discrimination under these Acts are against the law.

Direct discrimination is when someone is treated badly simply because of their sex, colour, race, nationality or ethnic origin – for example, if a company refuses to give a woman a job because she has children, but does employ men with children.

Indirect discrimination is when certain conditions are unfair for some people – for example, if a job involves wearing clothes that cannot be worn by people of a particular religion.

* The Disability Discrimination Act 1995 makes it illegal for an employer to treat a disabled person less favourably than a person without that disability for a reason that relates to the person's disability.

Activity

1 Prejudices are challenged by organisations that try to change people's attitudes. Look at the three postcards. The first was produced by the Disability Services department of Queensland Government in Australia. The last two were produced by the Commission for Racial Equality.
   a) For each card, say what the prejudice might be.
   b) How is that prejudice being challenged?
   c) Do you think that challenging prejudices can change people's attitudes?
2 Work with a partner. Design a postcard to challenge prejudice against young people.

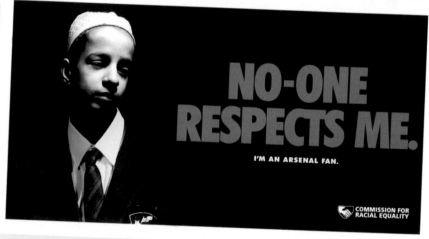

Prejudice and discrimination

The equal opportunities laws were brought in to stop people treating others unfairly by discriminating against them. Discrimination means stopping someone from getting a job, a home or some other benefit because of prejudices.

When people make a judgement about someone without knowing that person, it is called prejudice. In other words, they 'prejudge' a person because of their age, sex, race, disability, social class, accent, size . . . whatever. Most people have prejudiced attitudes – some negative, some positive. For example, we may think that all grey-haired elderly ladies are law-abiding.

Activity

Look at the cartoons below and decide what prejudice is being shown.

2.6 Access for all?

Many people with disabilities feel that they are denied the right to participate fully in society because their access to public places and workplaces is restricted. This may prevent them getting to the places as well as getting into them.

Activity

Look at the illustration below.

1 Identify all the things that might make moving around and getting into places difficult for people with disabilities. As well as wheelchair users, consider people who use walking aids and those who are deaf, blind, or have other impairments.
2 Identify the things that have been done to improve access.
3 What do you think still needs to be done to make sure public places and workplaces are accessible for disabled people?
4 How accessible is your school?

'Access denied'

Changing attitudes towards people with disabilities can be just as important as removing physical barriers to access.

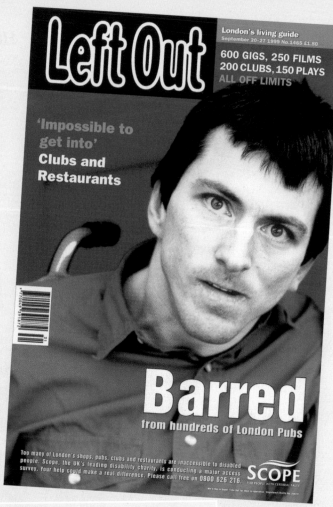

London's living guide
September 20-27 1999 No.1465 £1.80

Left Out

600 GIGS, 250 FILMS
200 CLUBS, 150 PLAYS
ALL OFF LIMITS

'Impossible to get into' **Clubs and Restaurants**

Barred
from hundreds of London Pubs

Too many of London's shops, pubs, clubs and restaurants are inaccessible to disabled people. Scope, the UK's leading disability charity, is conducting a major access survey. Your help could make a real difference. Please call free on 0800 626 216.

SCOPE FOR PEOPLE WITH CEREBRAL PALSY

Activity

1 Read the quotations below.
2 What do they show you about attitudes towards people with disabilities?
3 What do you think are the main ways in which this situation can be improved in shops, transport and public places?
4 Choose one of the quotations and write a letter of complaint to the organisation involved.

A 'This clothes store opened recently and I wanted to look around. Unfortunately, disabled people's needs have not been considered by the people who designed the layout of the store. It is impossible to go between the rails in a wheelchair or to reach anything. I find clothes get caught on the handles of my chair. The cash desk is too high to reach in comfort and the changing rooms are impossible to get into.'

B 'I was recently called for jury service but was not allowed to take part. I am deaf and in order to serve on a jury I would require a British Sign Language interpreter . . . Even though we challenged the decision the court ruled that a thirteenth person could not be allowed into the jury room.'

C 'In the past I have felt patronised and demeaned by shop assistants who seemed to look at me as if there was no point in disabled people wearing make-up. But this year it was a real pleasure to shop for make-up and perfume . . . The sales staff took time to listen to me and were not put off by my difficult speech. What a joy!'

D 'I love clubbing – getting in, having a beer and having a laugh. I love the atmosphere and chatting to people, especially women. Sometimes I have trouble getting into clubs – bouncers turn me away and it's really annoying because they won't give me a reason. Sometimes they tell me to come back on a quiet night. But why would I want to go when it's not pumping?

I recently went to Freedom at Bagleys in London and had a great time – it was really casual and laid back. Once inside it was really accessible with ramps between dance floors. Getting into the club involves stairs but I had the best service I have ever had from bouncers – two guys carried me up all the stairs in my chair.'

From *Left Out, disabled people's access to goods and services* by Gwilym Morris and James Ford, published by Scope

A question of words: does language matter?

One difficulty facing people with disabilities is the impact of the negative words used to describe them. The use of negative words affects the way that the people using those words think about the people they are describing. Some of the words are simply offensive: 'freak', 'cripple', 'spastic'. But some, which used to be considered acceptable, are now seen as negative. The word 'handicapped', for example, comes from a time when disabled people had to beg 'cap in hand' to survive.

Words can make disabled people appear as victims. We may say that disabled people 'suffer from' a disability or are 'afflicted' by one. We may say we 'admire' 'brave' disabled people for being 'plucky'.

Disabled people do not want to be pitied or admired. They do want to take part in all the things that non-disabled people take for granted: the cinema, restaurants, sports, bars, public transport.

Sandy Blythe

SANDY BLYTHE, CAPTAIN OF the Australian men's wheelchair basketball team, doesn't like the title of the *Herald's* previous Paralympic supplements 'The Brave Games' one bit. 'Patronising, ignorant and insulting – do you want me to go on?' he says.

Blythe admits to being thoroughly sick of labels in general. 'First I was an invalid. Then I was crippled. Then handicapped. Now I'm disabled.' The disability is always seen as central to the person. 'I mean, when did you last see a disabled person in an advertisement where the disability is either irrelevant or incidental?' he asks. 'It doesn't attract sponsors to be seen as "plucky".'

Swimmer Brendan Burkett says that whenever he meets people, their initial focus is on his disability. 'They look at you and see something different,' he says. 'But once they see us perform, they focus on the sport. They see how exciting it can be and they tend to forget about everything else. They see us as athletes ...'

Priya Cooper, another swimmer, agrees that patronising attitudes still exist. 'I can see that people think we're brave, and there's that stuff about the Brave Games, but it's not really. We're not brave,' she says. 'Anyway, attitudes are changing. It's definitely getting better. People are realising that we have to do the same things as able-bodied athletes – that we have to train and work hard and ... well ... it's not just training, it's a lifestyle.'

Sydney Morning Herald, Tuesday 2 May 2000

Activity

1 Read the article from the *Sydney Morning Herald*.
   a) What does it tell you about the way disabled athletics have been presented in newspapers and other media?
   b) According to Sandy Blythe, how has he been labelled in the past?
   c) Why do you think the three sports people here object to people only seeing 'the disability'?
2 Why do you think many disabled people do not like the words in the box being applied to them?

| brave   plucky |
| handicapped |
| courageous   retarded |
| helpless   afflicted |
| struck down   unsightly |

Activity

Read these three case studies. Work in pairs.

1 You are a radio interviewer. Draw up a list of questions you would like to ask two of the people featured here.
2 Put together a five-minute radio broadcast about the issues that face disabled people. Use material from pages 30–35 to put together information, statements by disabled people and interviews with disabled celebrities. You can find a lot of extra information about disability on the internet.
3 Invite some disabled people into your classroom to talk about their lives and ideas. You could include their contributions in your radio item.

TANNI GREY-THOMPSON

Paralympic gold medallist

Tanni Grey-Thompson, who has spina bifida, first started to take wheelchair racing seriously as a teenager and has excelled in the sport for more than a decade. She has won the London Marathon four times, and five golds and three silvers in the Paralympics at Barcelona 1992 and Atlanta 1996. She came home from Sydney 2000 with four golds ... and received an OBE in the 2000 New Year's Honours List.

Tanni says Sydney was a turning point, not just for her, but for disability sport as a whole. 'For me, Sydney was fantastic. It was the coming of age for disability sport.' Certainly the UK took the Paralympians to their hearts in a big way. The tabloids were full of letters praising their sporting achievements ...

Beneath her slight and elfin-faced exterior is a steely, competitive and successful young woman. 'I am competitive by nature, always have been. I was like it from about the age of five or six, wanting to win anything,' she says ... It was her parents' determination to treat Tanni the same as any other child that she has to thank for her indomitable nature, she believes. 'My parents were really positive. Their support influenced all my attitudes. They told me "If you want to do something you can do it, we're not treating you any differently."'

CRAWFORD CARRICK-ANDERSON

Mountain bike racer

One of the UK's top mountain bike riders, Crawford Carrick-Anderson from Edinburgh, is deaf. Crawford, 21, is a downhiller — the strange sport of heading, as fast as possible, down a mountainside obstacle course on two wheels. It's a sport that's high on adrenalin, strong on image and full of attitude. Whilst riding for the Clan Downhill Team, and becoming British Senior Series Winner in 1998, he caught the eye of his present sponsors, Giant UK ...

Crawford manages to communicate with other riders. 'I can communicate with my team mates and other

'I've been lucky,' she admits. 'I had access to a good education and I haven't had a discriminatory upbringing. I just grew up not tolerating it.'

riders, but it's not 100 per cent. When I meet a new face it's difficult, but after a few hours we can understand each other.'

His deafness can be an advantage: 'At the race I can focus myself because I can't hear anything. At the start I don't get distracted by the chatter which goes on.'

FRANCESCA MARTINEZ

Stand-up comic

Since winning the Daily Telegraph Open Mic Award at the Edinburgh Festival in August 2000, stand-up comedienne Francesca Martinez is seriously hot property. Slim, attractive and already exuding star quality, 23-year-old Francesca certainly has plenty to say. 'It all went crazy after Edinburgh,' she admits. 'My act really struck a chord somewhere. I think it's because I am a woman with cerebral palsy [CP] who speaks openly and honestly. People find that an eye-opener because I deal with it head-on and I pair disability and humour together.'

Francesca's act draws heavily on her disability ... However, she is keen to stress her individuality rather than her membership of the group 'disabled people'. Her past as a pupil at a mainstream school in west London, successful actor in TV's *Grange Hill* and model has all helped shape a view of the world based on a strong sense of self and a tendency to avoid the 'herd' mentality.

'I'm not talking about an issue, I'm just talking about my life,' she says. 'Society's ignorance does tend to lump disabled people together when, in fact, we're all individuals. It's as bad as saying that people who can't dance should be called "can't dance people". Most disabled people I know would agree that they want to be seen as individuals. Disability is not like any other minority group because it spans all races and genders, and anyone can become disabled at any time. People shouldn't always marginalise and assume "they all think the same". I have no knowledge, for example, of what it's like to have restricted growth.'

But Francesca is happy if her success means she is a role model to young disabled or able-bodied people and helps address some of society's prejudice. 'If I inspire someone, that's wonderful. But I hope I inspire them because I am following my dreams, not because I've got CP.'

2.8 Human rights under British law

The European Convention for the Protection of Human Rights

The Council of Europe was formed in 1949. European countries came together after the Second World War to try to prevent a European war ever happening again. After the horrors of the Nazi regime in Germany – the murdering of millions of Jews, and hundreds of thousands of gays, Gypsies and disabled people, the use of torture and forced labour – the countries also wanted to set up a code of rights that all European countries should respect. The Council based its code on the Universal Declaration of Human Rights agreed in 1948 by all the countries that had joined the United Nations, and called it the European Convention for the Protection of Human Rights (ECHR).

The Council of Europe set up the European Court of Human Rights in Strasbourg, where individuals from member states on the Council could bring cases if they thought their human rights had been violated. Here citizens could go above the heads of their own governments.

However, it was later decided that the rights in the Convention should become part of the law of each member country (see page 22).

The articles in the Convention
The list below summarises the European Convention for the Protection of Human Rights.

* Article 1: Introduction
* Article 2: Everyone's right to life shall be protected by law.
  – *Designed to stop governments and authorities killing people because they are troublesome; also raises questions about euthanasia (mercy killing) and life-saving medical treatments.*
* Article 3: No one shall be subjected to torture or to inhuman or degrading treatment.
  – *Raises questions about areas such as the treatment of prisoners, adults hitting children and the treatment of refugees.*
* Article 4: No one shall be held in slavery or made to do forced labour.

* Article 5: Everyone has the right to liberty and security of person.
  – *Aimed at preventing authorities keeping people in prison without proper trial.*
* Article 6: Everyone charged with a crime is entitled to a fair and public hearing within a reasonable time by an independent and impartial tribunal established by law. Everyone shall be assumed innocent until proved guilty and shall have a lawyer to speak for them.
  – *Means that courts and judges should be independent of (not taking orders from) the government.*
* Article 7: No one shall be subject to retroactive penalties or law.
  – *Means that people should not be convicted of a crime that was not a crime when they did it.*
* Article 8: Everyone has the right to respect for their private and family life, home and correspondence.
  – *Raises questions about how far authorities can intrude into the private life of people, e.g. prohibiting gay relationships, tapping phones, barring parents from seeing children, using surveillance equipment in childcare cases and benefits claims.*
* Article 9: Everyone has the right to freedom of thought, conscience and religion.
* Article 10: Everyone has the right to freedom of expression.
  – *Means that people can voice their views even if unpopular; allows journalists to criticise government; does not mean people can say anything they want, as incitement to violence and race hatred is against the law.*
* Article 11: Everyone has the right to freedom of peaceful assembly and to freedom of association with others, including the right to form and join trade unions for the protection of their interests.
  – *Allows people to meet together to exchange ideas and protects the right of people to hold peaceful protests.*
* Article 12: Men and women of marriageable age have the right to marry and have a family.

* Article 1 of Protocol 1 (added later): Everyone is entitled to the peaceful enjoyment of their possessions.
* Article 2 of Protocol 1: No person shall be denied the right to education.
* Protocol 6: Abolition of the death penalty.

Prejudice and discrimination

* **Prejudices** are opinions that we form without knowing all the facts or much information. They are attitudes.
* **Discrimination** means treating someone unfairly because of your prejudice. It is an action.

Many prejudices are harmless. But prejudices are harmful if people are treated unfairly because of them. Treating people unfairly because of prejudice against their sex, race or disability is called discrimination.

Disability Discrimination Act 1995

This Act covers in detail several areas of discrimination against people with disabilities. To summarise:

1 It is unlawful for a provider of goods and services (e.g. a shopkeeper or pub owner) to discriminate against a disabled person:

* by refusing to provide the same goods or services that they would normally provide for other members of the public
* by charging a disabled person more for goods or services
* by providing a worse standard of goods or services.

2 The Act aims to ensure access for disabled people to:

* places which members of the public enter, e.g. shops, cinemas and council buildings
* information in different formats, e.g. providing books in braille, hearing loops or a signer so that hearing-impaired people can participate in, for instance, council meetings

* free services, e.g. libraries and advice centres
* doctors, hairdressers and dentists
* insurance and financial services.

The Act is being changed to cover more areas.

Disability Rights Commission

This was set up in 2000. Its role is to champion disabled people's rights, to tackle discrimination and to secure equal opportunities. It aims to achieve 'a society where all disabled people can participate fully as equal citizens'. It offers:

* a helpline
* an information and advice service
* advice to the government on policies to do with disabled people.

The law about race

* In the UK, the **Race Relations Act 1976** makes it illegal to discriminate against anyone because of their race, colour, nationality or ethnic origin. This applies to jobs, training, housing, education and the provision of goods and services.
* The **Race Relations (Amendment) Act 2000** strengthens the 1976 Act. It places a new duty on public authorities to promote equality of opportunity and good relations between people of different racial groups.
* Racial violence is a criminal offence, as is inciting or encouraging racial hatred. This means that if you are found guilty you are a criminal and can be sent to prison.
* Racial prejudice is not against the law because an attitude cannot be made illegal.
* The **Commission for Racial Equality** was set up in 1976 to tackle issues of racial discrimination across the UK, to work for racial equality and to encourage good relations between people from different racial backgrounds. It receives money from the government.
* There are also just over a hundred **Racial Equality Councils** around the UK that tackle racial discrimination and try to encourage good relations in local communities.

The laws on sex discrimination

Two Acts cover sex discrimination. These are the **Sex Discrimination Act 1975** and the **Equal Pay Act 1970**.

The Sex Discrimination Act 1975 prohibits sex discrimination against individuals in employment, education, and the provision of goods, facilities and services. It also prohibits discrimination in employment against married people. The Act applies to women and men of any age, including children. Discriminatory advertisements are also unlawful, but only the **Equal Opportunities Commission** can take action against advertisers.

There are some exceptions to the law. For example, in recruitment, some jobs can be offered only to men or only to women. These would include parts in plays and films; where the job requires living in; where the job requires privacy; or where the job requires supervision of people of the same sex.

The Equal Pay Act 1970 gives an individual the right to the same pay and benefits as a person of the opposite sex in the same employment, where the man and the woman are doing similar work or work of equal value.

Running debates

* You need a 'motion'. Motions are worded in a particular way: e.g. *'This house believes* that bullies should be suspended from school every time they bully someone.'
* Two people should speak 'for' the motion. Each speaker has a limited amount of time to make a case. The second speaker should add something new to the case, not just repeat what the first speaker said.
* Two people should oppose the motion, again speaking for a limited time.
* During the debate a chairperson calls people to speak and makes sure they stick to the time limit given to them.
* Speakers can be interrupted during their speeches, but only in two ways:
  1 If someone thinks the speaker is off the point, they can call 'point of order'. The chairperson asks the challenger to say what the point is and decides whether or not it is valid.
  2 If someone wants to ask a question or add some information, they can call 'point of information'. The speaker decides whether to allow this person to interrupt.
* When all speakers have finished, the debate is 'opened to the floor' so that others can express their views. Anyone wanting to speak tries to catch the eye of the chairperson. The chairperson decides who should speak.
* After an agreed period of time a vote is taken. You should vote 'for' the motion, 'against' the motion or you can 'abstain' (not vote for either side). The votes are counted and the motion is either 'carried' or 'defeated'.

section 3

Local government and community
How can you have a say in local decisions?

Key words
- community involvement
- Council Tax
- election
- police
- political party
- protest
- services

Sometimes people like the area they live in: they feel they 'belong', they may have lots of friends who live nearby. Sometimes people don't like the area they live in: they may feel alone and that nobody cares about them. To some extent this depends on what the area has to offer – schools, libraries, shops, cinemas, clubs, housing estates, good transport, leisure centres, the way the streets look, how clean or dirty they are, and so on.

The local council provides many of the services mentioned above, such as libraries, collecting rubbish, council housing, making the area pleasant to live in. People pay a Council Tax to the council and the councillors and council officers spend it on the services they think local people want. If the services are not working properly people need to know how to contact the council to get them improved. If we want to change the area in which we live, we have to learn how to work with the council to make this happen. If the council does things we don't approve of, we need to know how to persuade it to change its mind.

People shouldn't leave everything to the council. There are lots of things people can do to improve their local area. They can get involved in community activities, help other people and join groups that aim to improve services and facilities.

In this section you will learn about:

* the services provided by the council
* who pays for the services
* ways that you can get involved
* ways of protesting about things you don't agree with
* voluntary organisations in your community.

You will:

* analyse information
* discuss your ideas
* present and explain your ideas
* make decisions
* present ideas you may not agree with
* use your imagination to consider how other people might feel.

3.1 What's the local area like ... and how can you improve it?

1 Study the picture carefully.
   a) Find five things about this town centre that would make people feel it is not a pleasant place.
   b) Find three things that people would like about it.

2 Which of these things are similar to your nearest town centre?

3 Find a map of your town centre, or a local centre if you live in a big city. Mark on the map the things you like and the things you don't like about it. You can find maps on the internet.

4 Your class could take photographs showing the good and bad points about the town centre. Make a display of these with captions for each photo.

Activity

1 **What do you think could be done to improve the town centre you looked at on pages 40 and 41?**

2 **Who should improve the local area? Which of the statements below do you agree with?**

> We pay the council to do it. It should be left to them.

> I didn't cause all the mess, so it's not up to me to do anything about it.

> Everyone feels better about living in a place that looks clean and cared for. If we want a nice environment to live in, then we'd all better help.

> We can help by not making a mess in the first place.

> There are lots of volunteer groups who can do it.

> The government should give us lots of money to make the town centre a nicer place.

3 **Now think about the area you live in. List five things you would do to improve your nearest town centre.**

Town meeting

Gradsworth is a small town that is planning to develop its town centre. Four proposals have been put forward (see below and opposite). It has decided to begin by calling a consultation meeting. It has invited along representatives of some of the main groups interested in the changes being proposed. The groups at the meeting are:

* councillors
* The Gradsworth Society
* religious leaders representing Christian, Jewish, Muslim and Hindu faiths
* the Residents' Action Group
* the Chamber of Commerce
* the Youth Action Group
* the police
* a transport group representing buses, taxis and delivery vans.

Divide the class into groups of three or four. Each group will take the role of one of the groups above. These are described in detail on pages 44–45.

There are four proposals to be discussed:

1: Hostel for homeless men

Homeless men have been a serious problem in and around Gradsworth for some time. A number beg on the streets and some have been aggressive. The place suggested for the hostel is an old church and its hall which have been closed for several years. It is a residential area.

Proposing: Religious leaders
Against: Residents' Action Group

2: Traffic congestion

The number of cars, buses, lorries and taxis passing through the centre of Gradsworth has increased enormously in recent years. There is terrible traffic congestion at some times of the day and air pollution is very bad. The council proposes to pedestrianise the town centre and re-route traffic.

Proposing: Councillors
Against: Transport group

3: Nightclub

In the evenings the centre of Gradsworth is like a ghost town. There is hardly anybody around because there is nowhere to go – the one small cinema is on the outskirts of town. A former pop star wants to open a nightclub/café in the centre catering particularly for young people.

Proposing: Youth Action Group
Against: Police

4: Shopping mall

There has been a market in the centre of Gradsworth for years, but it now sells mainly cheap, poor-quality goods. The old market building – the Exchange – is run-down and the market space is rough asphalt where cars park when the market is not on. There has been a proposal to put a new shopping mall on the site – a modern, enclosed building with spaces for shops and a food court.

Proposing: Chamber of Commerce
Against: The Gradsworth Society

* Read your role brief carefully and work out your views about the proposals (see pages 42–43). Think about what your group might say at the meeting and provide as many reasons as you can why you support some proposals but not others. You can develop the brief as you wish.

* Each group will be asked to speak for or against one proposal, but will also be asked its views on the other ones.

At the meeting

The meeting will be conducted by a neutral chairperson. This person will call the meeting to order and then announce the first proposal. The chairperson will call on the proposer and give them three minutes to present their arguments. Then the main group against will be given three minutes to make its points. After this the other groups can contribute their views.

There are only fifteen minutes in total to discuss each proposal. Then a vote will be taken by a show of hands to see if the meeting is generally for the proposal or against it.

The Gradsworth Society

The Society is made up of people who want to preserve the heritage of Gradsworth and protect old buildings, some of which have been neglected. You oppose the new shopping centre because you believe it will ruin the centre of Gradsworth. The market has been there for hundreds of years and could be improved if the council invested money in it. There could be a weekly farmers' market for local produce. A new shopping centre will mean demolishing some old houses – all for some modern monstrosity that will have the same shops as you see all over the country.

You are very worried by the pollution and damage being caused by vehicles going through the town centre and you therefore support pedestrianisation.

Religious leaders representing Christian, Jewish, Muslim and Hindu faiths

For some time the different religious groups have been working together to improve the lives of the less fortunate members of the Gradsworth community. You particularly want to help homeless men because there are a lot of them and they cause problems. Many people want to push them away, but you want to help them to get their lives in order. The disused church and hall would make a perfect hostel.

You are all worried about the idea of a nightclub. You feel it might lower the morals of young people as well as causing trouble and violence late at night.

Chamber of Commerce

You represent the small businesses in Gradsworth – retailers (e.g. clothes and bicycles), food outlets and other businesses such as the computer store and driving school. You are anxious to get rid of the old market as its stalls sell low-quality goods, taking away some of your members' business. You think a new shopping centre will help you to bring more people into the town and improve its image. However, you want to make sure that the rents will not be too high, so that your members will be able to rent shop space in the centre rather than all the space going to the big chains of shops.

You oppose pedestrianisation because you think it will stop people coming to the centre to shop and will make it difficult to deliver supplies to shops.

Councillors

You believe that pedestrianising the town centre will bring lots of benefits: less pollution; reduced traffic congestion; a safe, pleasant environment for local people; a chance to develop shops and cafés.

You are also in favour of the new shopping centre: you feel it will bring life and lots of shoppers to the town centre and some big stores will help to pay for road improvements.

The council will build several car parks as part of both schemes.

You have mixed feelings about the nightclub. You want something for young people but are worried about disruption.

Transport group

Your group is made up of the bus services, taxi drivers and delivery services. The bus services in Gradsworth are run privately. You are all worried by the proposal to pedestrianise. The bus company fears that people will travel by car to the town centre and park in the new car parks instead of using buses. Taxi drivers fear they will not be allowed into the centre to pick up people. Delivery drivers believe it is going to make their work more difficult.

You are, however, in favour of the new shopping centre and the nightclub because you think both will bring you lots of extra business.

Youth Action Group

You have formed a group for two main reasons. Firstly, you want to persuade the council to provide something for young people to do, particularly in the evenings. At the moment they just hang around the streets. You think the nightclub/café is a great idea – just what the town centre needs.

The second area you are interested in is the environment. You therefore support the proposals to pedestrianise the town centre. And you would like to see much more done for young people as part of the new plans.

Police

You are very worried about the proposed nightclub. It will bring to the town all the things you have so far avoided – drugs and lots of young people out on the streets throughout the night. With your manpower already stretched, you are not certain you can police this properly. If the nightclub does go ahead, you want more resources and you want strict limits to the club's licence.

You are also concerned about the hostel for homeless men. This might attract men that you consider to be undesirable and there might be a violent reaction from local residents.

Residents' Action Group

You have come together especially to fight the proposed hostel for homeless men. You do not think it is appropriate for the hostel to be sited in an area where many families with young children are living. You are concerned about child safety, unpleasant behaviour, possible violence and rowdiness.

You support the plans to pedestrianise the town centre as it will make it safer for children and probably more attractive. You are also in favour of the new shopping centre because you will be able to get easily to a range of shops in one big building which is protected from the weather. This is particularly attractive to parents with young children.

3.2 Do you get what you pay for?

What do you know about the services in your local area?

Think about the services in the area where you live. Make a copy of the chart below and complete it by answering these questions:

1 What services are provided in your area? *Put a tick against each one in the first column.*
2 Do you or your family use the services? *Put a 'yes' or a 'no' in the second column.*

3 Who provides the services? *Are these council services or are they provided by private companies or organisations?*
4 How good do you think these services are? *Rate them using the following scale:*
   1 = terrible   2 = poor   3 = good
   4 = very good   5 = excellent

Use the empty boxes at the bottom of the chart to add any other services in your area. The list on Info page 59 will help you.

Services	Is this service provided?	Do you or your family use them?	Who provides them – council or private?	How would you rate them on a 1–5 scale?
Rubbish collection				
Schools				
Looking after elderly people • meals • care				
Leisure centres				
Parks				
Childcare/nurseries				
Library				
Noise control				
Recycling centres				
Special events such as firework displays or local fairs				
Car parks				

You could use this chart to carry out a survey of your family and other adults to find out what they know about local services and what they think about them.

Who pays for the services?

Who pays for
your library?

Who pays for the
upkeep of your park?

Who pays the people to collect your rubbish?

The simple answer is – you do! Or rather your parents and guardians do. Every household (with a few exceptions) has to pay *Council Tax*. The tax is paid to the local council, which provides the services in the area. It is important to know about how your council spends money because it is your money, and the quality of your local services will have a big effect on what it is like to live in your area.

This pie chart shows how one council divides its money between the different services. You can get information about your area from your local council. Ask at the town hall or check the council website.

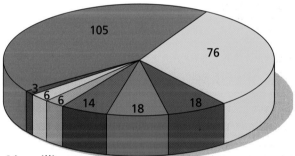

£ in millions
Figures rounded to nearest million

Key

- Education
- Social Services
- Housing
- Recreation
- Highways (roads)
- Environmental health
- Planning and economic development
- Refuse collection and disposal

Activity

1 **In the pie chart, what is the biggest proportion of the money spent on?**
2 **What is the smallest proportion of the money spent on?**
3 **Does either of these surprise you?**
4 **Do you think the council should have to pay for the police or the fire service?**
5 **Choose one category that you would spend a lot more money on. Explain how you would spend the extra money, and why.**

Example of council spending in a borough within a big city, 2001–2002. The council also spends nearly £70 million on individual projects such as repairing and doing up council houses and flats, improving schools and leisure centres and new sports facilities. It also has to pay around £150 million to the authority that runs the whole city for the police, fire service and transport services.

How would you spend the money?

You have looked at how you would like to see council money spent. But it is not always as straightforward as it seems.

1 Work in groups of five or six. You are a council committee that has been given the task of dividing up £100,000 between six competing demands. How are you going to spend the money? Will you allocate most of it to one cause or are you going to divide it up between several? Which ones are going to lose out?

2 When each group has decided how it is going to divide up the money, get the whole class together and see if you agree. Argue in favour of your group's decisions. This means you have to justify them.

3 What do you think this exercise tells you about the problems facing councils when they must decide how the money that they have collected should be spent?

1: Speed bumps

Two streets are regularly being used as 'rat runs' by motorists trying to avoid traffic jams. They are speeding down the streets, ignoring whatever signs you have put up. Two children have been killed in the past two years and several people injured. You could install speed bumps and chicanes to slow the cars down. This will cost £50,000.

2: Playground

The local park is in a poor state. There are now many parents with young children in the area. They could really do with some new playground equipment: a slide, swings and a sandpit. This will cost £40,000.

3: Library

The library needs some new children's books and some compact discs for the record library. They estimate that the cost will be £10,000.

4: School roof

The roof on a local primary school is causing a great deal of concern. For some time it has been letting in rain. The council building unit has had a look at it and says that there is a danger that it will collapse. Repairs to make it safe and last for about five years would cost £20,000. Or it could be replaced for £45,000 and last for the next forty to fifty years.

5: School equipment

A school which has been set up for children with physical handicaps is desperately in need of equipment When the council set up the school it promised that it would put in the equipment as soon as money became available. The estimated cost for this is £20,000.

6: CCTV cameras

There have been a large number of robberies in the high street quite near to the town hall. These include attacks on several old people after they had collected their pensions. The police say that CCTV cameras would dramatically reduce this problem. To install these cameras and link them to screens in the police station will cost £30,000.

How much do you pay?

People who live in council houses and flats pay a proportion of their rent as Council Tax. People who live in rented houses and flats have to pay the Council Tax on the property as if they owned the house.

For people who own their houses, the amount is set every year according to the value of the house. Each house is fitted into a band according to what its market value (how much it will sell for) was in 1991. The bands are the same across the whole of the country but the local council sets the amount of tax payable in each band. For example, a house in band A (valued up to £40,000) situated in Devon would mean a payment of £434 per year, whilst in Leeds a house in band A would mean a payment of £535 per year. An adult living alone gets a 25 per cent discount.

Band (house value in 1991 in £)		Council tax		
		Devon (£)	Richmond upon Thames (£)	Leeds (£)
A	Up to 40,000	434	606	535
B	40,001–52,000	506	707	623
C	52,001–68,000	579	808	713
D	68,001–88,000	651	909	802
E	88,001–120,000	796	1110	980
F	120,001–160,000	941	1312	1159
G	160,001–320,000	1086	1514	1337
H	320,001 or more	1303	1817	1604

Council Tax, 2001. (All figures are rounded to the nearest pound)

Activity

1 Calculate how much Council Tax each household pays.
2 Do you think:
   a) anybody is paying too much tax?
   b) anybody is paying too little tax?
3 Do you think the system is fair or unfair?
4 If you think it is unfair, can you think of any fairer ways for councils to get the money they need?

Mrs Biggins, aged 92, lives in Richmond on her own in an old rambling detached house. She receives the state pension and a small private pension which enables her to get by. But she has not been able to spend much on the house which now needs a lot of repairs. She is attached to her house because all her memories are there. Because of the high value of houses in her area it is valued at £520,000.

The Prestons live in Leeds in a large house with five bedrooms, valued at £220,000. They bought the house many years ago when it cost much less. The Prestons are not very well off. Mr Preston works, but his wife is not well enough to work. They have two children who are just finishing their education — one is doing her A levels and the other his GCSEs.

Mrs Jackson lives in Taunton, Devon, in a three-bedroomed house valued at £80,000. She lives with her three children from two marriages. All the children are over the age of eighteen and they all work. The eldest, Josie, is 27 and has a very well paid job in the computer industry. Mrs Jackson works full-time in a primary school.

Rajit and Parul Desai live in a three-bedroomed house in Leeds valued at £66,000. They have one child but expect to have more soon. Rajit is an electrical engineer. Parul is a primary-school teacher. Their joint income allows them to live comfortably.

John How lives in Exeter, Devon, in a one-bedroomed flat valued at £41,000. He works for the Post Office on the counters dealing with the public. His salary is not very high.

Jane and Christopher Crochett live in Richmond in a small terraced house with two bedrooms, valued at £300,000. They live there during the week because they work in the City of London. Christopher is an accountant; Jane is a solicitor. Their combined salary is over £200,000 per year. At the weekends they go to their second home in Devon, a five-bedroomed detached house valued at £180,000. They only have to pay half the council tax on this because it is not their main home.

3.3 Can you change anything?

If people don't think the council is spending its money wisely or providing good-quality services, they can vote for a different council at the local election. But this only comes around every few years. There may be things that the council is doing that you don't approve of or things they are not doing that you feel they should. All sorts of problems crop up – noisy or violent neighbours, road accident blackspots, new building developments – that people want the council to deal with. What can you do to change what's going on in your neighbourhood?

Activity

Working in pairs, look at the issues below. These issues might occur in any local area. Can you as an active citizen do anything about them?

Look at the What could you do? box on page 53 and decide which course of action you think is appropriate in each case. Use your own ideas as well when deciding what could be done.

A Your rubbish is not being collected regularly.

B The local primary school is being closed to save money.

C Some neighbours in your area are very noisy. A young man down the road often plays music until 3 a.m.

D A new supermarket is being built where the old market used to be. You think the council has done a deal with the supermarket to get money for developing new roads. The local people do not want another supermarket. You want a leisure centre or a skating rink.

E The council has agreed to allow a land developer to remove a large number of ancient trees which were part of the common land near where you live. This is a site of great natural beauty with rare butterflies.

F A particular place where people cross the road (there is no alternative) has been the scene of a number of accidents. You have begged the council to put in a proper pelican crossing, but nothing has been done. After the latest accident, in which a girl broke her leg, you agree with other local people that something has to be done.

What could you do?

This list shows some of the things you could do to tackle these issues. Some of the issues are more important or serious than others, so the courses of action you might take would vary accordingly. Be careful – the last three on the list are illegal. They are there because some people do take illegal action in response to problems and you need to discuss whether this is ever justified.

1 Ring up the council and talk to the official responsible.

2 Write a letter of complaint to the council.

3 Go to see your local councillor. They usually hold regular 'surgeries' to listen to the complaints and problems of the people in their area.

4 Draw up a petition to send to the council.

5 Write to the local newspaper if the council does not respond.

6 Organise a local demonstration or march in connection with the issue. Invite the local newspaper along and invite local councillors to join you.

7 Take part in peaceful but disruptive behaviour, e.g. sitting down in the road, occupying houses or areas of countryside.

Illegal

8 Damage property to make people take notice of your views.

9 Be violent towards a person you think is responsible for the problem.

10 Plan a campaign of fear and intimidation, with others, against the group of people you hold responsible.

G The council has decided to open a house in your area for men who have just been released from prison. They have all served sentences and are not regarded as presenting any danger to the local community. They all have jobs to go to. This is a 'half-way house' to help the men back into normal society.

H The council has granted planning permission to a medical company to build a laboratory. The company uses animals in experiments to test medicines.

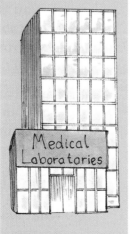

Discuss

1 Come together as a whole class and compare the decisions you reached about the various issues. Discuss the reasons why you decided one course of action was preferable to another.

2 Which issues did you think were serious enough to take strong action?

3 Do you think any issues justify breaking the law?

4 Do you think that violent action can ever be justified as a way to express your views about local matters?

5 Which of these statements do you agree with? Why?

① It's important to be actively involved in local matters because these are the things that affect our lives.

② It's not worth bothering with local problems. The council always does what it wants anyway. Nobody listens to local people.

What do you do with your waste?

Even when a council provides a service, the success of the service can depend on local people – on us! One example is the recycling of waste. We are all aware that waste is a problem.

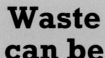

Buried in landfill sites

Waste is packed in layers and compressed, then covered over.

Advantages
● Relatively cheap and easy to do

Disadvantages
● Can create unwanted methane gas and pollute groundwater
● Uses enormous amount of land
● Special taxes are making it more expensive

Waste can be

Incinerated

Waste is burned in special centres.

Advantages
● Huge bulk of waste reduced
● Can be used where levels of groundwater are high
● Heat generated can be used to heat homes
● If done properly it is hygienic

Disadvantages
● Ashes and gases can be released which are harmful to people's health and the local environment
● Is expensive
● People don't want incinerators near where they live

Dumped at sea

Waste is taken out into the open sea and thrown in.

Advantages
● Cheap

Disadvantages
● Pollutes the sea and kills fish

All of these methods are BAD for the environment but we will always produce waste and it has to go somewhere.

Discuss

1 Which of the three main ways of disposing of waste do you think is the most acceptable option?

2 How would you feel if the council decided to:

• build an incinerator near to your home?

• open up a landfill site near to your home?

3 What effect would these have on your lives and what would, or could, you do about it?

Recycling

Recycling some of our rubbish helps to reduce waste. Councils now *must* provide collection points for some rubbish – e.g. paper, glass, metal, plastic, cloth, cardboard. Some councils are doing a great deal to encourage people to recycle their waste.

Reducing and reusing

Recycling is not the only way we can help the environment by reducing the growing mountain of waste. We can also cut the amount of waste we produce and we can reuse many items. For example:

Reduce

We can:

* stop buying food (including fast food) with so much packaging
* use cloth nappies instead of disposable ones
* use china plates and metal cutlery instead of plastic ones
* compost most garden and kitchen waste.

Reuse

We can:

* reuse plastic carrier bags
* take old clothes and shoes to charity shops so someone else can use them
* use glass milk bottles
* use washable bottles and flasks for drinks instead of throwaway cartons.

Did you know?

* The amount of waste paper buried in the UK every year would fill 103,448 double-decker buses.
* We throw away 28 million tonnes of rubbish from homes each year – the same weight as three and a half million double-decker buses.
* Each year food shops give away enough carrier bags to cover an area the size of London.
* We use up a forest the size of Wales to provide us with enough paper for just one year.
* Each day 80 million cans are buried in landfill sites – one and a half cans per person.
* Every day eight million nappies are thrown away. A child uses 5,580 nappies in its lifetime – weighing as much as a medium sized car!

Information from Waste Watch

Activity

1 **Look at the contents of the bag of rubbish above. How could a household dispose of some of these items in a way that is less harmful to the environment?**

2 **Choose one or two of the points in the 'Did you know?' box and use them to design a small poster encouraging people to be more environmentally friendly.**

In many places in Europe, particularly in Germany, households have separate containers for different types of waste. These are collected regularly by the local authorities.

Activity

1 Make a copy of the chart below. Tick the boxes to show whether you think the items can be thrown away, recycled, reused/reduced. Use the last column to explain how the items could be reused or reduced. Add other items to the chart.

	Throw away	Recycle	Reuse/ reduce	How to reuse/reduce
Old clothes		✓	✓	*Take to charity shop, hand down to smaller children, mend*
Glass bottles and jars				
Metal cans: – aluminium – other metal				
Plastic: – bottles – carrier bags – other				
Paper: – newspapers – envelopes – other				
Cardboard				
Toys				
Books				
Disposable nappies				
Autumn leaves				

2 Schools produce a lot of waste. As a class, draw up a plan for how you can reduce waste in your school, e.g. lunchtime waste (cans, cartons, food packaging), classroom waste (paper). Send your plan to your headteacher.

3 There are quite a lot of recycling sites around but not everyone uses them. Carry out a survey in your class. Find out how many people use the recycling sites and what kinds of waste they recycle. Everyone should answer truthfully the questions in a copy of the questionnaire below. You could also use a copy of the questionnaire with your families and people you know who live near you. You can add other questions if you like.

Recycling questionnaire

1 Do you ever recycle waste from home?   Yes No ☐ ☐

2 What do you recycle regularly?
   ✓
   a) paper   ☐
   b) glass   ☐
   c) metal   ☐
   d) plastic   ☐
   e) cardboard ☐
   f) cloth   ☐
   g) other   ☐

3 Do you know where your nearest recycling site is? Yes No ☐ ☐

4 Is it near enough to walk to?   Yes No ☐ ☐

5 If you don't recycle waste, what are the main reasons why you don't?
   _____
   _____

6 How could the council make it easier for you to recycle waste?
   _____
   _____

---

4 a) Gather together all the answers to the survey and make a big chart to show how people have responded.
  b) Write a report for the council explaining how people could be encouraged to recycle more waste. As a class, choose one report and send it to your local council.
5 a) Find out where the recycling points are in your area. The council will have maps showing the points, probably on its website. Mark all the points on a map.
  b) Mark other places where you think recycling centres would be useful.

Meet your local councillor

You have been doing activities about how local councils work and how they provide the services that determine what your area is like. You will have developed your own ideas and will no doubt have some questions to ask your own councillors and council officers.

The best way to find out what is happening in your area is to talk to the people who run your council. Invite some of them into school. Alternatively, you could write a letter to your local councillor asking any questions you may have about your local area and saying what you think about it. Here are some ideas about what you could ask.

* Look back through the activities in Section 3 and list any questions you would like to ask about:
  – improving the town centre
  – plans for developing your area
  – plans for young people
  – council services
  – waste, recycling and the environment.
* Put forward some of your ideas about how the local area could be developed and improved.
* You could carry out the Town Meeting on page 42 during the councillors' visit and ask them what would happen in real life.

If you choose to write a letter you could base it on the one on the right.

Alex Spring
Starcross School
Pentworth Street
Bristol
BR4 0T3

5 March 2003

Anthony Robinson
The Town Hall
Bristol
BR1 YT4

Dear Councillor Robinson,

I am writing to ask you a few questions about . . .

I think the new recycling facilities in Park Town are a good idea but they are too far away from our area. I propose . . .

I look forward to hearing from you about this.

Yours sincerely,

Alex Spring

3.4 Council services

Services provided by councils

Housing

* Maintainance and repair of council houses
* Provision of services on housing estates

Education

* Runs schools under the council's control
* Gives money to schools in the area
* Gives parents advice about schools
* Makes arrangements for pupils with special educational needs

Environmental services

* Street cleaning and rubbish collection
* Environmental health, including food safety and pest control
* Air quality, noise pollution (and noise patrol)
* Trading standards (making sure shops are selling safe products and not cheating people)
* Improvements to the area (changes to streets and buildings)

Leisure and amenities

* Parks and open spaces
* Recycling centres
* Recreation and sports centres
* Libraries
* Cemeteries
* Youth clubs and schemes for young people

Planning and technical services

* Gives permission for new building – houses, flats, offices or other business premises
* Housing improvement – gives permission to people who want to change their houses
* Highways and pavements, engineering works (e.g. digging up roads for pipes, putting in road humps, etc.)
* Crime prevention, including CCTV cameras

Social services

* Families and children
* Adoption and fostering
* Care of elderly people
* Young people who break the law
* Mental healthcare in the community

Council Tax

The amount of tax paid depends on the value of the property, which will fall into one of eight bands (A–H) as shown on page 50. The council decides the tax for each band. If people do not agree with the valuation of their property, they can appeal to have it put into a lower band.

If there is only one adult living in a property, the tax is reduced by 25 per cent. There are some circumstances where the reduction can be given even if there is more than one adult in the household. These are when the other adult is:

* aged eighteen but still in school
* under the age of twenty and a full-time student, trainee nurse, on a youth training scheme or apprenticeship
* a patient in hospital, or in a nursing or care home
* a carer for someone with a disability
* severely mentally impaired
* in prison.

Councils and waste

Councils are obliged to reduce and recycle waste. In 1996, the government introduced a landfill tax of £7 per tonne of waste, to stop councils sending so much of it to landfill sites and encourage them to persuade people to reuse and recycle waste.

In 2000, the government set councils targets for the recycling of household waste: 25 per cent by 2005, 30 per cent by 2010, 33 per cent by 2015.

Council elections

Local councils are elected. Each council area is divided into wards. The people who live in each ward elect the councillors. In country areas there is usually one councillor for each ward, but in cities and towns wards often have two or three councillors. A borough council in a city may have around 50 councillors elected from twenty wards.

All council elections take place on the first Thursday in May. Councillors are elected to serve for four years. Elections use the first-past-the-post system. This means the candidate with the highest number of votes wins. In wards which have, for instance, three councillors to represent them, the three with the highest number of votes are elected.

Some councils have big elections every three or four years to choose a new council. Other councils have elections every year to choose part of the council, usually between one-quarter and one-third.

The party with the most councillors is in charge of running the council. Sometimes no party has a majority, so parties have to work together. Not all councillors belong to the big political parties – Labour, Conservative, Liberal Democrats. Some belong to smaller parties, like the Greens, or are independent (belong to no party at all). Councillors are not paid, though they receive expenses for attending meetings.

To become a councillor you must be 21 or over and live in the area of the council you want to be on. Some categories of people, such as many council employees, are not allowed to stand. You become a candidate for a 'ward' (see page 59).

What work does a councillor do?

The council
All the elected councillors and some senior council officers meet around once a month to discuss issues affecting the local area and to decide what to do about them.

Committees
Most of the detailed work is done in council committees. A small number of councillors sit on a committee, which overlooks the work of a particular department and decides the policy of the department. Council officers also sit on the committee to give information and advice. For example, the Planning Committee makes decisions about which housing developments should be allowed to go ahead. Some very important decisions have to go back to full council.

Meeting local people
Councillors hold **surgeries**, where local people can go to discuss their problems with their councillor. These might include problems on their housing estate, dirty streets or the lack of nurseries in the area.

Running a meeting
The chairperson is very important. He/she must make sure that:

* the meeting gets through all the items
* people who want to speak get a turn
* people obey the rules of debating and do not interrupt each other
* decisions are reached on each item, if possible
* everyone knows what will happen as a result of the decision.

The chairperson *must not* take up time in the meeting giving his/her own opinions. Whether or not the chairperson agrees with what is being said, he/she must allow that person to speak. Anyone wishing to speak should raise a hand, but can only speak if the chairperson says so (or the speaker for points of information, see page 38).

At the beginning of each item, the chairperson should ask for a short introduction from the person who is proposing the item. When people have had their say about the item, depending on the time available, the chairperson should call for a vote.

section 4

Central government and Parliament
How does politics work?

Key words
- authoritarian
- campaign
- collective responsibility
- constituency
- democracy
- election
- manifesto
- motion
- Parliament
- political party
- pressure group

The UK is a democracy. This means that the national government is chosen by the people of the country in a general election. If the people are not happy with the government it can be voted out at the next election. All democracies have laws to protect the rights of people in those countries, such as freedom of speech and the right to a fair trial.

Not all countries in the world today are democratic – some have authoritarian governments. This usually means that a ruling group makes all of the decisions. The people of the country have to do as they are told. They can be treated unfairly and unjustly, their rights are not protected by law, and there are no elections. People can be put in prison if they oppose or criticise the government.

In UK elections, people vote to choose a Member of Parliament to represent their locality in the House of Commons. A Member of Parliament almost always belongs to a political party. The party that wins the most seats in the House of Commons in the election forms the government. But other parties also have Members of Parliament. The job of the whole of Parliament is to make laws, discuss important issues and keep an eye on the government, to make sure it is running the country properly.

We all like to think we live in a free country. But it is important for people to know how our democracy works and how we can keep it. In the past, a lot of people fought hard for the right of all adults to vote and to have a say in the way the country is run. If nobody cares about freedom, we could easily lose it.

In this section you will learn about:

* political parties and what they believe in
* what goes on in Parliament
* how decisions are made
* how people can make their voices heard
* general elections
* what it is like to live in an autocratic country.

You will:

* analyse information
* present your opinions and justify them
* take part in group discussions
* think about and explain views that are not your own
* use your imagination to consider other people's experiences.

4.1 Political parties

A political party is an organised group of people with a leader and members. It stands for something – it has a set of views that the members agree with. Parties put up candidates at elections so that these people can be voted into positions of power, nationally or locally. People join a political party because they agree with what it stands for. They also want to help the party to win elections and put their ideas into practice.

Activity

You are going to create your own political party.

1 Work in groups of four or five. Imagine that you want to make the country a better place in which to live. What would you change? In your group, choose three things that you would like to change. You can get some ideas from this page, or you can come up with some of your own.

Clean up the environment

Ban smoking in public places

Make the health service better

Make sure everyone can get a job

Provide more social services to help people

Help poorer people in the rest of the world and refugees

Cut down crime

Build more houses for people who are homeless

Stop people claiming benefits they are not entitled to

Bring in laws to protect animals

Improve schools

Get rid of traffic jams

2 Give your party a name and elect a leader.

Our party is suggesting a number of ways to improve the environment in which we all live.

3 a) Decide what you want to do about the three issues you have chosen. These are your *aims*.

b) Decide how you are going to do it. These are your *policies*.

4 Draw a chart like the one on the right, and fill it in. (The completed row is just an example to help you.) When you have done this, you have written the party *manifesto*.

Name of our party:		
Our three issues	What we want to achieve (our aims)	How we can do it (our policies)
Get rid of traffic jams	Encourage more people to use public transport (trains and buses) instead of cars. Get lorries off the road by transporting more goods on the railway.	Charge people big taxes for driving cars in cities. Make public transport cheaper and quicker. Make rail transport of goods very cheap.

5 When you have agreed your policies, you have to convince other people that you are right. You have to plan your *campaign*.

a) Discuss how you can persuade other people to agree with your views.

b) Design campaign posters and put them up in the classroom.

c) Write a leaflet to give to people. You could use a computer to help you design and print it.

d) Write a three-minute speech for the leader of the party to give to the whole class. Invite some visitors to listen to the speeches. Your visitors can vote on which party was the most persuasive.

Political parties in the UK

We hear about the main political parties all the time because they are in the news: the Labour Party, the Conservative Party, the Liberal Democrats. There are, however, many political parties that we hear less about. The following political parties all have Members of Parliament:

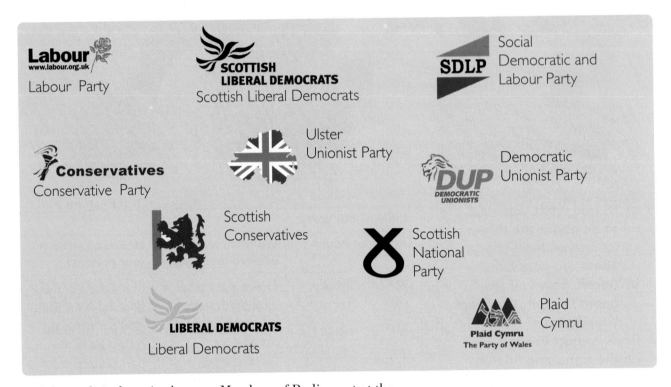

Other political parties have no Members of Parliament at the moment. Some of them are quite small. The British Register of Political Parties lists 110 organisations! Look at the logos of just a few:

Have you ever heard of any of them?

The three main parties

What do you know about the three biggest political parties: Labour, Conservative and the Liberal Democrats?

1 Work in groups. Make three lists, one for each party. Write down words and names that you associate with each party. Think about famous party leaders and ex-leaders, policies, emblems, colours, words and ideas. Use the words below and the pictures to get you started. You can find more help on Info page 84.

help poor and disadvantaged

City of London

Labour
www.labour.org.uk

Conservatives   civil liberties   socialist

Blair wins with New Labour

free market   yellow   upper classes   working classes

Lib Dems say 1p on income tax for education

freedom of the individual   red

LIBERAL DEMOCRATS

middle classes

trade union

business

NHS

blue

proportional representation   low taxes

2 These three short extracts (right) come from the websites of the three main parties. Match each extract to one of the parties.

3 Write to local branches of the three biggest political parties and ask them for information about their policies.

A We believe that people should be involved in running their communities and are determined to ensure that there is a just and representative system of government.

B It's 100 years since our party was set up to fight for representation for trade unions and socialist societies in Parliament.

C We intend to ensure that Britain is the best place to do business, the best place to live and one of the most admired and influential countries in the world.

And the winner is...

There are 659 Members of Parliament, one for every *constituency* in the country. At election time, the winning political party is the one that wins most seats in the House of Commons. That party forms the government. Sometimes the government has a large majority and sometimes the majority is very small. The party with the second largest number of seats is the *official opposition*.

The government needs an overall majority in the House of Commons to pass laws and win votes. The overall majority is the difference between the number of seats held by the biggest party (the government) and the number of seats held by all the other parties put together. If the government does not have an overall majority it has to do deals with other parties to get laws passed.

Activity

Look at the results of recent general elections (below) and decide, in each case, which party was in government, and which party was the official opposition. How big was the overall majority in each election?

1992 (There were 651 seats in 1992)		**1997** (The number of seats increased to 659 because of boundary changes)		**2001** (659 seats)	
Conservative Party	336	Conservative Party	165	Conservative Party	166
Labour Party	271	Labour Party	418	Labour Party	413
Liberal Democrats	20	Liberal Democrats	46	Liberal Democrats	52
Ulster Unionist Party	13	Ulster Unionist Party	10	Ulster Unionist Party	6
Scottish National Party	3	Scottish National Party	6	Scottish National Party	5
Plaid Cymru	4	Plaid Cymru	4	Plaid Cymru	4
Others	4	Others	10	Others	19

Recent general election results.

Activity

a) **By how many votes did Lorna Fitzsimons (Labour) win over her nearest opponent? (This is called her *majority*.)**

b) **How many people voted for all the other candidates?**

c) **Do you think it is fair that Lorna Fitzsimons got elected?**

How people voted in one constituency in June 2001

Rochdale

Lorna Fitzsimons (Labour Party)	19,406
Paul Rowan (Liberal Democrats)	13,751
Elaina Cohen (Conservative Party)	5,274
Nick Harvey (Green Party)	728

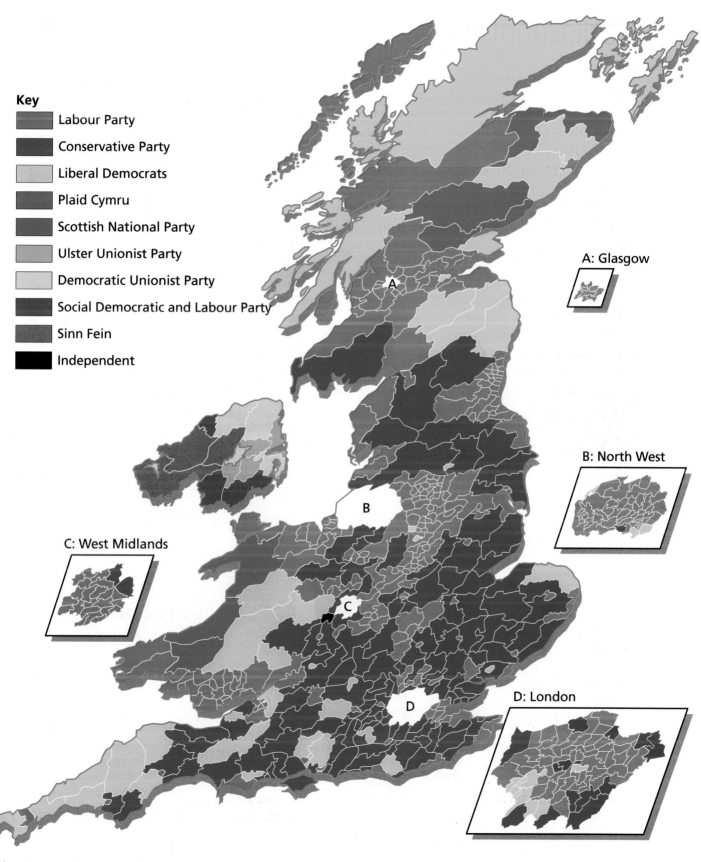

Key

- Labour Party
- Conservative Party
- Liberal Democrats
- Plaid Cymru
- Scottish National Party
- Ulster Unionist Party
- Democratic Unionist Party
- Social Democratic and Labour Party
- Sinn Fein
- Independent

A: Glasgow

B: North West

C: West Midlands

D: London

The 659 constituencies following the election in 2001. Each constituency has about 67,000 voters and is represented by one MP.

4.2 How do you become a Member of Parliament?

All citizens of the United Kingdom over the age of 21 are eligible for election to Parliament, unless they are, or have been, in prison, have certain kinds of mental illness or are members of the House of Lords.

You could be an MP when you are older. Most MPs are members of political parties, although there have been some famous 'Independents' who have won a seat without the help of a party.

Wyre District

Dr Richard Taylor was the only Independent MP elected in the 2001 general election. His campaign was fought on the single issue of saving services at Kidderminster Hospital and demanding the re-opening of its accident and emergency department.

He won a majority of nearly 11,000, getting a huge 58 per cent of the vote.

Martin Bell was a famous Independent Member of Parliament. He was a correspondent for the BBC and had travelled to many war-torn countries, reporting

TATTON
CONSTITUENCY

for the television news. He was horrified by the behaviour of one Conservative MP who had been accused of taking bribes. Martin Bell challenged the MP in the 1997 election. He won the seat, saying that he stood for 'anti-sleaze'.

Activity

These pictures show the stages in becoming an MP but they are in the wrong order. Put them in the correct order. If there are any words you don't understand, you will find them explained on Info pages 84–86.

A
Anna Cassidy joins a political party. She works for the party for several years: attending meetings, helping out at election time, canvassing, raising funds for the party.

B
After the vote has ended, the ballot box is taken to a hall with all the other ballot boxes in the constituency. The votes are counted. The Returning Officer then announces that Anna is the candidate with the most votes. She is now the MP for her constituency and will go to the House of Commons.

C

Anna has an agent to run her campaign; he organises posters, leaflets and public meetings. Party volunteers help her by putting up posters, etc. They canvass for her; this means they go round houses in the constituency asking the voters to vote for Anna and her party. They explain what Anna and her party stand for and the policies in the party manifesto.

D

The day of the election arrives. The voters go to a polling station. They are each given a ballot paper with the names of the candidates on it. They take their paper to a polling booth where no one can see what they are writing. They put an 'X' next to the candidate they want to vote for. Then they put their ballot paper in a sealed metal box.

E

After a number of years Anna decides that she wants to be an MP. She puts her name forward for an interview with the constituency selection committee. Several other people are also interviewed. She is chosen to be her party's candidate at the next election.

F

The Prime Minister decides that it is time to call an election. The Queen dissolves Parliament and the election campaign starts.

4.3 Get it sorted! Run a class election

Who would like to be voted an MP in your class election? Divide the class into two: one half will be candidates and helpers, the other half will be voters. Candidates and helpers should follow the instructions in the yellow panel. Voters should follow the instructions in the blue panel.

CANDIDATES AND HELPERS

■ Five or six members of this group will be the candidates. Each candidate should have one or two helpers.

■ The candidates will need to meet to decide which parties they will each represent. Three candidates should represent the main parties, others the smaller parties or made-up parties with their own manifesto.

■ Candidates and helpers should work out their manifesto together. Each manifesto must state what the party will do about:
  ■ education
  ■ transport and roads
  ■ health.
  Ideas for other policies can also be added.

■ Each candidate will have to have a plan of campaign – for example, posters and leaflets. One helper should be chosen as campaign manager. Helpers can also make rosettes.

■ Candidates will need to visit the voters and talk about what they will do if they win and to try to persuade voters to vote for them. Journalists will expect to be able to interview candidates.

VOTERS

● The voters should form groups of three. These groups should then decide what they want the candidates to do about the following issues:
  ● education, e.g. provide more teachers, reduce class sizes
  ● transport and roads, e.g. get rid of traffic congestion
  ● health, e.g. provide more doctors and nurses.
  Two more issues should be added to this list.
  Spend 15–20 minutes on this.

● Voters should now get into two larger groups.
  ● **Group One** is in charge of the election. One member of the group should be elected Returning Officer to make sure everything is fair. The group should design and make enough ballot papers for everyone in the class to use, including the candidates and helpers. A sample ballot paper is shown opposite. This group should also make or find a ballot box to put votes in.
  ● **Group Two** is made up of journalists who are following the campaigns and reporting what is going on. They could do this by writing headlines to pin on the class noticeboard (e.g. 'Conservative candidate promises tax cuts'). Journalists will be interested in any scandal surrounding a candidate. They will also want to interview candidates, and the voters in Group One. A list of questions should be put together before the interviews begin.

Voting will take place at a pre-agreed time. Everyone has a vote, including the candidates and helpers, and the vote is secret. Each voter should have a ballot paper. Mark a cross against the chosen candidate, fold the paper and post it in the ballot box.

Sample ballot paper.

Candidates	**X** Mark a cross against your chosen candidate
BROWN, Sam (Monster Raving Loony Party)	
JONES, Frankie (Conservative Party)	
MACDONALD, Angus (Independent)	
PATEL, Rehanna (Liberal Democrats)	
ROBERTS, Chris (Labour Party)	
SMITH, Alex (Green Party)	

The Returning Officer and the rest of Group One should make sure that the count of the votes is fair. Journalists could also keep an eye on things. The count should be carried out in public so that everyone can see it. The Returning Officer announces the result to the class. The results should be read out as shown in the example below:

I [*name*], being the Returning Officer for Class *X* do hereby declare that the votes cast by Class *X* in this election are as follows:

Brown, Sam	10 votes
Jones, Frankie	3 votes
MacDonald, Angus	2 votes
Patel, Rehanna	6 votes
Roberts, Chris	2 votes
Smith, Alex	5 votes

I therefore declare that Sam Brown is duly elected as Member of Parliament for Class *X*.

The winner should then make an acceptance speech.

4.4 Putting pressure on politicians

Each Member of Parliament has a vote on every *motion* discussed in the House of Commons. To decide how to vote, MPs will think about:

* what their political party says on the issue
* their own opinion
* the views of the people they represent
* the views of other important groups.

These other important groups are sometimes called *pressure groups*. Pressure groups are organisations of people who have strong opinions on a particular issue. They try to influence what happens by putting pressure on the people who make decisions. Pressure groups don't want to stand in elections or form parties in Parliament. They just want their views to be taken into account. Sometimes they are fighting for their own rights and sometimes for the rights of others.

Activity

Here are some examples of pressure groups. Which of these, do you think, are fighting for their own rights, and which are fighting for the rights of others?

Greenpeace

Help the Aged

Road Haulage Association

The National Union of Teachers (NUT)

The National Association for the Care and Resettlement of Offenders (Nacro)

Campaign for Nuclear Disarmament (CND)

British Medical Association (BMA)

National Society for the Prevention of Cruelty to Children (NSPCC)

Amnesty International

Royal Society for the Prevention of Cruelty to Animals (RSPCA)

Pressure groups want to influence the government, Members of Parliament and public opinion. They do this in lots of different ways.

Activity

Look at the pictures below and describe the different ways pressure groups try to get their message across.

No smoke without fire

Imagine that the House of Commons is going to vote on whether to ban smoking in all public places, e.g. restaurants, bars, clubs, pubs, buses, trains, theatres or cinemas. Smoking would only be allowed out of doors or in someone's home.

There are lots of pressure groups that would try to influence how MPs voted. They would have different views about this issue. You can see examples on the opposite page.

Fifteen members of the class will be Members of Parliament. The MPs should work in groups of three and each group should sit at a separate table. They should decide what the arguments are *for* and *against* banning smoking in public places. Below are a few ideas to help.

This is a free country. I can smoke wherever I like.	Smoking is a form of relaxation. It helps me to enjoy my evening.	Smoke from other people's cigarettes gets into my clothes and makes them smell.
I don't want to breathe in other people's smoke. It makes me cough.	If I don't allow smoking in my pub, people will not want to come here.	There is a huge cost to the health service from smoking-related illnesses.
People should be discouraged from smoking because it is bad for them and for others around them.	There should be some smoking and some non-smoking areas in all public places.	People often complain about smokers at the next table in my restaurant. It would be easier if no one smoked at all.
Lots of people have jobs in the tobacco industry. If we reduce smoking, they will lose their jobs.	Tobacco growers often come from poor countries that will become even poorer if fewer cigarettes are bought.	There are too many laws saying what we can and can't do already. Adults should be able to decide for themselves.

The rest of the class should divide into five groups. Each group should take on the role of one of the pressure groups. You can see a summary of their views on the opposite page.

In your pressure group, decide how you are going to try to persuade the MPs that they should vote your way. Spend some time getting your arguments clear. Some of the arguments in the boxes on this page may help you.

Now visit the MPs, one group at a time. Only visit groups of MPs when they are not being visited by another pressure group. You must try to convince the MPs by the power of your arguments. Move round after three minutes, or when the teacher says.

When every pressure group has visited every group of MPs, the MPs should hold a vote on whether to ban smoking in public places. If they are in favour of the ban, they should go to one part of the classroom, and if they are against it, they should go to another part. In Parliament, when MPs vote, they go through different doors to the lobby outside the Commons chamber. They are counted as they go through the door.

Here is a summary of the views of the pressure groups.

ASH

ASH was set up in 1967. It is against smoking in public. It represents non-smokers' rights and often fights cases against the tobacco industry in court. It wants to see more non-smoking areas and it wants all tobacco advertising banned. It also wants to encourage people to give up smoking. If smoking is banned in public places, ASH thinks more people would give it up.

FOREST

FOREST was founded in 1979 to defend the rights of adults who smoke tobacco and to fight discrimination against smokers. FOREST does not promote smoking in any way. It has never denied that there are health risks in smoking. But it claims that it is up to the individual to decide whether or not they want to smoke: it is a matter of individual freedom, not for the government to decide. FOREST provides information about how the needs of smokers and non-smokers can be met.

The BMA

The BMA represents doctors and other medical staff. Its main concern is that smoking causes lung cancer and is a major cause of ill-health. It is worried about the dangers of 'passive smoking' (breathing in the smoke from other people's cigarettes). It has called for a ban on smoking in public places and, in particular, in the workplace. It also wants to clamp down on sales of tobacco to children.

The hotel and catering industry

The people who own restaurants, cafés, bars and pubs are part of the catering industry. This group is worried that people will not go out to eat and drink if they cannot have a cigarette, or that they will stay for less time and spend less money. The loss of money could bring about staff cuts. The industry also makes money from sales of tobacco and cigarettes.

Tobacco industry workers

Workers in the tobacco industry are worried that their jobs will disappear if many people stop smoking or smoke less. The workers' group argues that people should be allowed to choose how they spend their own money. It also points out that the government makes a lot of money from taxes on tobacco. These taxes can be spent improving the health service.

Discuss

1 Which arguments were the most powerful in persuading the MPs how to vote?
2 How else, apart from face-to-face argument, might the pressure groups have tried to change opinions?
3 Some pressure groups have more money than others to spend on persuading people of their point of view. Is this unfair?

4.5 What does the Cabinet do?

The Cabinet is the top government committee. It is made up of ministers who run the big government departments (see below). It has regular meetings at which all the most important issues facing the country are discussed. It also talks about foreign affairs and the problems of other countries in the world and how these might affect the UK.

The Cabinet does not usually make important decisions. But all the members of the Cabinet have to agree to support the policies that the government decides to adopt. This is called *collective responsibility* – all of them are responsible for the government's actions. If things turn out badly, none of them can later say that they really disagreed with the policy and that it was nothing to do with them.

One of the big issues the Cabinet talks about is the economy: how can they make sure that businesses do well and that there are plenty of jobs, that people have money to spend on goods and can afford to buy or rent houses. The government also has to decide how to spend all the money it collects from taxes. It is often the way the government runs the economy and spends money that determines whether or not people are happy with a government.

There are usually between 20 and 22 members in the Cabinet. Different governments sometimes change the way the jobs are described. Some of the most important Cabinet posts can be seen.

How powerful is the Prime Minister?

The Prime Minister (PM) is the head of the government. The PM chooses the ministers in the Cabinet when he or she forms a government after a general election. The PM is the chairperson of the Cabinet and co-ordinates the work of the different government ministers. The PM should work with the Cabinet to discuss key issues. In recent years people have said that the PM tends to make all the important decisions, and is becoming very powerful while the Cabinet is becoming less important.

Minister for Defence responsible for making sure that the United Kingdom is well defended in case of attack by other countries; also in charge of funding the army, navy and air force

Minister for Social Security responsible for benefits of all sorts, e.g. unemployment benefit and pensions

Minister for Transport responsible for building roads, dealing with issues to do with public transport and also for airports and air safety

Foreign Secretary speaks for the United Kingdom in its dealings with other countries

Prime Minister

Minister for the Environment responsible for looking after the environment and reducing pollution on land and in rivers and seas

Activity

Cabinet ministers argue for more money to spend on their departments and areas of responsibility. Look at the speech bubbles on the right and match each one with the Cabinet member who you think might have said it.

Home Secretary responsible for running the police force and the prisons, for law and order in the country and for overseeing the system of justice

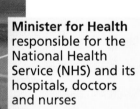

Minister for Health responsible for the National Health Service (NHS) and its hospitals, doctors and nurses

Chancellor of the Exchequer responsible for managing the finances of the government – how much is collected in taxes and how much is spent

A There have to be more constables on the streets, visible to the public. We need at least another 20,000 police constables. And the latest report shows that our prisons are in a terrible state.

B The army needs new tanks, the navy more ships and submarines and the air force new planes. We need weapons with the latest technology, so that we don't fall behind other countries.

C You all want more money for your departments. But where is all the money going to come from? We will have to raise taxes. I have to balance the budget – you can't spend more money than people pay in taxes.

D Everybody knows that we have to improve the trains and buses if we want more people to get out of their cars and use public transport. It will take a huge amount of money to bring our transport services up to the level of other European countries.

E We need better equipment and modern hospitals to serve our people. We need to train more doctors and more nurses.

F The only real way to help the pensioners is to put more money in their pensions.

G If we are going to protect the landscape and reduce pollution from cars and industry, then we will have to spend substantial amounts of money to improve transport and pay farmers to look after the countryside.

A taxing problem

Governments need money to spend on schools, the armed forces, building projects and many other things. Cabinet ministers are in charge of spending money in their departments, e.g. the minister in charge of health spends money on hospitals, doctors and nurses. The money to pay for these things comes from the taxes that people pay.

The problem is that there is never enough money to pay for everything.

One way of dealing with this problem is to cut the money given to some areas to give more to others. Would you:

* cut the money for the health service
* cut the money for weapons for the armed forces
* save money by recruiting fewer police officers?

It is not an easy decision, is it? The alternative is to raise taxes, but people don't like having to pay more in taxes. And if the government makes them pay too much, it might lose the next general election.

> **There are two main types of tax**

Direct tax

Income tax
This is a tax on the money people earn. It is called a progressive tax, because the more you earn, the more tax you pay. Here is a simplified example.

Income (£)	Tax (£)
First 5,000	No tax
Band 1 5,001–10,000	10% (you pay £10 tax in every £100 you earn)
Band 2 10,001–30,000	20% (you pay £20 tax in every £100 you earn)
Band 3 Over 30,000	40% (you pay £40 tax in every £100 you earn)

National Insurance
This is a fixed percentage that people pay towards the National Health Service and as insurance in case they become unemployed.

Profits of companies
Companies pay a percentage of their profits to the government.

Indirect tax

This is a tax on the goods and services that people buy. Everybody pays the same amount of tax.

Customs and Excise duties
Payable on petrol, alcohol, cigarettes, new cars.

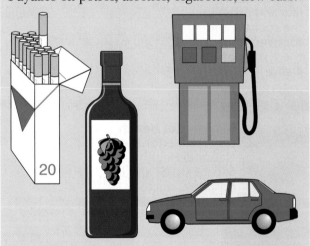

VAT
Value Added Tax is paid on goods and services. People who do building repair jobs or car repairs charge VAT on their work. At the moment it is 17.5 per cent, so a decorator who charges £100 for a job would add on £17.50 VAT.

Activity

1 The government has to think about the impact any changes in tax might have on different groups of people. Suppose the government was thinking about:

* raising income tax payable in Band 2 to 25% and Band 3 to 45%
* increasing the tax on alcohol and cigarettes
* increasing VAT to 20%
* increasing the tax companies pay.

Look at the people below. Work out:
a) how the changes might affect them
b) which changes they would not like.

2 Which do you think is the fairest way of raising money – imposing direct or indirect taxes?

Reginald Jones is a businessman. He runs a medium-sized company specialising in computer equipment. He started the company in his own repair shop and has built the company up from nothing. He now earns £80,000 a year and is convinced that the taxman already takes too much of his hard-earned money. His company is doing well, but he has to compete with companies in other parts of the world and does not want to see any tax increases on his business as it will make his computer products more expensive. If this happens he might have to lose some workers.

Betty Goddrich lives in a rented flat. She looks after her two children on her own. She has a job in a bakery in a town about twenty miles away. The only way she can get there is to use a car. Her overall earnings are just over £12,000 a year. She is finding it hard to make ends meet. The price of goods is very high and her car is expensive to run. Her flat needs repairs that she cannot afford to have done. Her only small pleasures are a drink in the evening and a few cigarettes.

Fiona Bruce is a teacher. She lives with her husband, also a teacher, and their two children in a house on the outskirts of a city. She earns around £25,000, as does her husband. They each have a car to take them to their schools, which are quite a distance away. They are having a lot of building work done at the moment. They are having a new kitchen put in and the roof repaired. They enjoy a few glasses of wine after a hard day at school.

Jai Singh is a car mechanic. He works long hours but earns good money – around £26,000. He lives in a flat on an estate with his wife and small child. He needs all the money he makes to pay the mortgage on the flat and buy the furniture and kitchen equipment, e.g. washing machine, to make it nice. He does not smoke or drink or spend much money other than on his family.

4.6 What sort of government would you choose?

Your country has just lost a long war. All the old rulers and the old system of government have been thrown out and you have the chance to start afresh. You can choose the way you want your country run. However, you have to take the state of the country into account.

State of the country

Although the war is over, your country is in a terrible mess and likely to be so for several years:

* Many people are desperate – they are poor and hungry and large numbers of them cannot get jobs. They have to rely on the charity of others.
* In some parts of the country, law and order has broken down and armed gangs are taking control.
* There is fighting on the streets between rival political groups who want to run the country.

Work in groups of three or four. Your group has to make decisions on the nine areas shown below and opposite. Make a copy of the table on the right and record on it whether you choose 'a' or 'b' in each case. Try to agree on decisions and make notes about those points on which you cannot agree.

	Decision 'a' or 'b'
1 Type of government	
2 Political parties	
3 Law and justice	
4 Police	
5 Freedom of speech	
6 Freedom of association	
7 The press	
8 Other media	
9 Attitude to foreigners	

1 Type of government

Choose either:

a

a strong ruler and his or her supporters to run the country and restore law and order. Elections to take place at some later date. ▲

or

b

a government elected by all the people of the country. Elections to take place at regular intervals, so that the people can change the government if they don't like what it is doing. ●

2 Political parties

Choose either:

a

people to be able to join different political parties and choose who to vote for in elections. ●

or

b

only one party so that there is less argument and the country will be united. ▲

3 Law and justice

Choose either:

a

a system of laws that apply equally to everybody in society and by which everybody is entitled to a fair trial. ●

or

b

laws that apply to everybody but sometimes people can be arrested and sent to prison without a trial in the interests of keeping control. ▲

4 Police

Choose either:

a

a police force that is independent (separate) from the government.

●

or

b

a police force that is run by the government, carries out its orders and arrests people who oppose the government.

▲

5 Freedom of speech

Choose either:

a

the government to control what people can say.

▲

or

b

everybody to have the right to say what they think.

●

6 Freedom of association

Choose either:

a

people to be prevented from forming associations because it leads to disagreements, trouble and fighting between different groups.

▲

or

b

people to be able to form groups and associations whenever they want with people who share similar political views, e.g. trade unions.

●

7 The press

Choose either:

a

journalists with freedom to write what they want in newspapers and magazines.

●

or

b

the government to be able to stop journalists criticising it by censoring anything it does not like.

▲

8 Other media – TV, cinema, radio

Choose either:

a

media that can broadcast and show whatever programmes they want.

●

or

b

media controlled by the government who decides which programmes are suitable. 'Unsuitable' programmes could include those showing life in other countries, or those with a sexual content.

▲

9 Attitude to foreigners

Choose either:

a

to keep foreigners out because they might take jobs and bring in ideas and values that are not wanted in the society.

▲

or

b

to welcome people from different races and religious groups into the country because they can bring new ideas and different views on many issues.

●

What sort of political system did you choose?

Below each choice ('a' or 'b') on pages 80–81 you will see a triangle or a circle symbol. Match these up to the choices you recorded on your table by putting a triangle or a circle next to each of your choices. Count up the number of triangles or circles you chose.

If you chose more circles than triangles, you favoured a more democratic system: elections, several political parties, rights for individuals.

If you chose more triangles than circles, you favoured a more authoritarian government: strong leader, one party, opposition controlled, few rights for individuals.

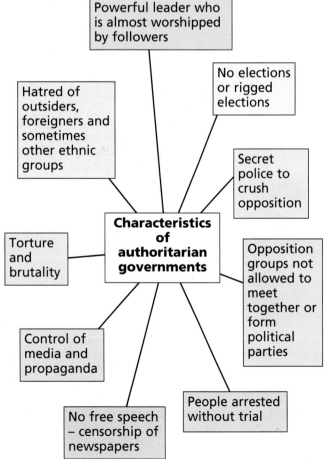

Powerful leader who is almost worshipped by followers

No elections or rigged elections

Hatred of outsiders, foreigners and sometimes other ethnic groups

Secret police to crush opposition

Torture and brutality

Characteristics of authoritarian governments

Opposition groups not allowed to meet together or form political parties

Control of media and propaganda

People arrested without trial

No free speech – censorship of newspapers

Authoritarian governments

The diagram below shows the main features of an authoritarian government. There are a number of ways in which such governments can come to power. Sometimes a group of people seize power and then force their ideas and their way of life on the rest of the people in the country. Sometimes governments are voted in and then become more authoritarian. But there are other occasions when people choose and support an authoritarian government, especially when times are difficult and people are desperate. This happened in Germany in the 1930s: many Germans voted for Adolf Hitler and the Nazi Party because their country was in a terrible state. They thought Hitler could solve their problems and make Germany a strong and united country again.

In a democratic society, people often think they will never lose their freedom. But circumstances can change, particularly when there are threats like terrorism or if there is a lot of violence and crime. Governments might want to introduce stricter laws to control people's behaviour or more surveillance to monitor what people are doing. The people may welcome these actions at the time but later an authoritarian government could use these powers against people and deny them their rights.

Discuss

Using the information in the text and the case studies opposite:

1 **Why do you think some people in a country might support an authoritarian government?**
2 **Why do such governments want to silence people who oppose them?**
3 **Why do they treat people in the ways described in these case studies?**
4 **Why do you think people oppose governments when the consequences can be so serious?**

There are many countries in the world today – in South America, in Africa, in the Middle and Far East – that have authoritarian governments. People in these countries, often with help from organisations outside, fight hard against these governments to force them to ensure that the people are given their basic human rights. Read the examples in the case studies below.

Case study 1: China

Zhang Lin is 36 and has campaigned for democracy in China since he was 18. He is a founder member of China's Democracy and Justice Party. He has already served five prison and labour camp sentences for his opposition to the Chinese government. He is now in Guanzhou No. 1 re-education camp.

He has been repeatedly tortured for his protests. His mother was beaten and threatened after she had written a letter of appeal which was published in the United States. She has been told that if she contacts the international media again she will never see her son again.

Case study 2: Togo

In 2000 a law was passed in Togo, West Africa, limiting press freedom and making it an imprisonable offence to print criticism of the government.

Lucien Messan is a journalist and editor of the Togolese newspaper, *Le Combat du Peuple*, which frequently challenges the government and exposes human rights violations committed by the state security forces. In June 2001 he was sentenced to eighteen months' imprisonment for 'forgery and use of forgeries'. However, human rights campaigners believe he was convicted because of his work as an independent journalist. Lucien is being held in Lomé prison where conditions are cruel, inhuman and degrading.

Case study 3: Dominican Republic

A trade union leader imprisoned in the Dominican Republic wrote: 'I was being kept naked in an underground cell. When the first 200 letters came, the guards gave me back my clothes. The next 200 letters came and the prison officers came to see me. When the next pile of letters arrived, the director got in touch with his superior. The letters kept coming, 3000 of them, and the President called me to his office. He showed me an enormous box of letters he had received and said, "How is it that a trade union leader like you has so many friends all over the world?"'

What can be done?

It may seem that you can do little when you live far away. But there are things you can do. Amnesty International has for many years campaigned on behalf of prisoners of conscience, journalists who have been arrested for speaking out against their governments and people who have been tortured or imprisoned without trial. It encourages people to write letters of support. And this can have an effect, as case study 3 shows. See the work of Amnesty on its website at www.amnesty.org.uk.

AMNESTY
INTERNATIONAL
UNITED KINGDOM

The main political parties

Labour Party

The Labour Party was formed in 1906. Its members came from the trade unions and its aim was to get representation in Parliament for working people. The Labour Party first won an overall majority in an election in 1945. It set up the National Health Service and other welfare benefits. In the early days, the Labour Party believed in state ownership of the big industries – coal, steel, transport. The Labour Party today believes much more in private industry and the free market. It still believes in helping everyone to get chances in life and in improving the welfare state. It broadly supports the European Union.

The Labour Party, Millbank Tower, London, SW1P 4GT. www.labour.org.uk

Conservative Party

The Conservative Party changed its name from the Tory Party in the nineteenth century. The Tory Party helped landowners and stood for their rights. However, today, the Conservative Party defends business enterprise and supports private ownership of property. It believes in reducing taxes and minimal government interference in the economy. The Conservative Party takes a strong line on law and order. It does not want to see further development of Britain's membership of the European Union.

The Conservative Party, 32 Smith Square, London, SW1 3HH. www.conservatives.com

Liberal Democrats

The Liberal Democrats were formed in 1989 when the Liberals joined with the Social Democrats, a breakaway group from the Labour Party. Before that, the Liberals were called the Whigs. The party supports the rights of individuals and believes strongly in civil liberties. It would like to see the voting system changed to 'proportional representation'. This means that the members of the House of Commons would be chosen more in line with how many people voted for them. The Liberal Democratic Party strongly supports British membership of the European Union.

Liberal Democrats, 4 Cowley Street, London, SW1 3NB. www.libdems.org.uk

Scottish National Party

The Scottish National Party was formed in 1934. It would like to see Scotland independent of the rest of the United Kingdom. It says that the natural resources (oil, gas, water) in Scotland should be used for the benefit of Scotland and not distributed to the rest of the UK. It supports higher spending on social services and education. It strongly supports the European Union and sees Scotland as a small country within Europe.

The Scottish National Party, 6 North Charlotte Street, Edinburgh, EH2 4JH. www.snp.org

Plaid Cymru

Plaid Cymru was started in 1925 and supports the Welsh language and culture. It wants Wales to be independent of the rest of the UK and to be a full member of the European Union. It supports greater public spending on health, welfare and education, and more government investment in transport, industry and agriculture.

Plaid Cymru, 18 Park Grove, Cardiff, CF10 3BN. www.plaidcymru.org

Who can stand as a candidate in a general election?

Any person over 21 who is a British or Commonwealth citizen, except:

* members of the House of Lords
* clergy
* bankrupts
* offenders sentenced to more than one year in prison
* patients held under mental health laws
* people whose jobs mean they should remain politically neutral, e.g. judges, members of regular armed forces, police officers.

Who is able to vote in parliamentary elections?

All British citizens over eighteen except:

* members of the House of Lords
* offenders sentenced to more than one year in prison
* patients held under mental health laws
* people convicted within the previous five years of illegal practices during elections.

Voting is not compulsory in this country.

What does an MP do?

An MP represents the people in his or her constituency in the House of Commons. The MP spends time in the local area:

* holding 'surgeries' where local people can talk about their concerns or problems
* visiting schools, hospitals, day centres
* listening to constituents' views, receiving and answering letters.

An MP goes to the House of Commons to:

* raise issues important to people in the constituency
* take part in debate
* make speeches
* ask the government questions
* represent their party on various committees.

An MP also travels:

* making speeches on behalf of the party in different parts of the country
* finding out more about particular issues in this country and abroad.

What is a constituency?

The United Kingdom is divided up into areas called constituencies. You live in a constituency and this is the area you vote in. One person is elected to represent each constituency in Parliament – an MP (Member of Parliament). In this way you also vote for the party which you wish to be in government. The different political parties put forward candidates and you have to choose one. The average size of a constituency is around 67,000 people.

How often do we have general elections?

The maximum life of a Parliament is five years. So there has to be an election at least every five years. A Prime Minister can call an election at any time during those five years, however, so there could be an election after three or four years. This is for the Prime Minister to decide, but it will usually be discussed with government ministers and people in the party.

What happens when the Prime Minister decides to call a general election?

The Prime Minister goes to the monarch (king or queen) to request that Parliament be dissolved (brought to an end). A Royal Proclamation is issued which allows the dissolution (ending) of the Parliament. General elections are usually held seventeen days after this.

The government

The Prime Minister is in charge of government. He or she chooses a group of people called the Cabinet to help run the country. The Cabinet is made up of the most important ministers in the government. They are in charge of the big departments such as the Foreign Office, Home Office (law and order, police and courts), Employment (jobs), Health (hospitals, doctors and nurses) and Education (schools and colleges). The Cabinet works with the Prime Minister to decide the government's major policies, for instance what it is going to do about schools, keeping law and order and health.

Civil servants help ministers run government departments. Civil servants are not elected. They work with the ministers from whichever party is in government. Their job is to carry out the government's policies. For instance, if the government decides to build more hospitals or more roads, they have to make sure this is done. The most important civil servants work with ministers to sort out the details of the policies and the best way of achieving the results the government wants.

Services provided by the government include:

* protecting the citizens – defending the country against attack by another country, keeping law and order, protecting consumers and protecting minority groups
* the welfare of citizens – health, social services, social security (e.g. unemployment insurance), housing and education
* the employment of citizens – creating jobs and providing training schemes
* looking after the environment – cutting down pollution, developing and improving the environment (e.g. in the countryside), preserving buildings of historic value or architectural importance, controlling the development of roads and housing
* running the economy – trying to ensure that people have work and have a reasonable standard of life, controlling powerful companies, giving money to certain areas to boost their economic performance.

Election glossary

agent   organises each candidate's campaign

ballot box   where ballot papers are put

ballot paper   paper with the names of all the candidates who want to be elected. Voters choose one by putting a cross next to the appropriate name

campaign   all the activities candidates and their supporters undertake to persuade people to vote for them

candidate   person standing for election as MP

canvass   asking voters who they are intending to vote for and trying to persuade them to vote for one candidate

constituency   area of the country, with around 67,000 voters, represented by one MP

deposit   to be put on the ballot paper, every candidate has to pay a deposit of £500. If they get more than five per cent of the votes, it is given back to them

dissolving Parliament   all MPs lose their jobs and the House of Commons is closed down until after the next election

electoral register   a list of the people who are entitled to vote

electorate   all the people who can vote in an election

general election   when people in all constituencies vote for their MP

opinion poll   poll carried out by telephone or in the street to find out the opinions of voters on particular issues and which party they are likely to vote for

polling station   the place where the voters cast their votes, usually a school or a church hall

Returning Officer   the person who is in charge of counting the votes in a constituency and declares who the winner is after the count

section 5
The media and society
What is news?

Key words
- censorship
- democracy
- fact
- news values
- opinion
- press freedom
- propaganda

The mass media includes television, radio, newspapers, magazines, films, advertising, popular music and the internet. These are different forms of mass communication that influence every part of our lives.

We learn about news and politics from the media. What we read, see and hear helps us to form our political opinions about important issues and events. Information about politics and the news comes to us from journalists. They play an important part in keeping everyone in a democracy informed about events. Journalists choose what news stories to write about in newspapers or to broadcast on television and radio. We call this 'news coverage'. They decide what to tell us about and what not to tell us about. It is therefore important that we should understand how they decide what news to cover and how they cover it. We need to think about what goes on behind the headlines and investigate how journalists select from all the events of a day to put together a ten-minute news bulletin or a newspaper front page.

Sometimes news stories reveal information about the private lives of individuals. The people in the news may be celebrities, criminals, victims of crime, politicians. Some journalists say the public has a 'right to know' about these people. Many people think they go too far in exposing private details. This is something else to think about. How far should journalists go?

In this section you will learn about:

* how news is 'managed'
* news values
* propaganda and 'spin'
* press freedom
* invasion of privacy
* the difference between fact and opinion.

You will:

* find out about how news is selected
* analyse examples of news
* discuss news in small groups and as a whole class
* make decisions
* give your opinion and explain it to others
* listen to other people's opinions.

5.1 What makes a good news story?

Most people follow the news every day, even if they only listen to the headlines on the radio between their favourite music programmes. Major events, such as train crashes, earthquakes, serious crimes or tragedies, are covered first and everyone knows about them soon after they happen.

But big stories don't happen every day, and broadcasters and newspaper journalists still have to fill news slots. So how do they decide what news to cover?

Activity

Look at this newspaper front page and discuss it with a partner.

1. What are the main stories?
2. Which one do you think is meant to be the most important? How can you tell?
3. Why was this one chosen as most important?
4. Why are the others also on the front page?

What's important: The Times, with more Sport, Business and Ne

Free film magazine

100-page Rough Guide to the Orange British Academy Film Awards

PLUS: the award-winning the times magazine

THE TIMES

70P

2W

www.thetimes.co.uk

SATURDAY FEBRUARY 23 2002

No. 67382

Pakistan urged to find Pearl killers

By Katty Kay, Zahid Hussain and Daniel McGrory

AMERICA is pressing President Musharraf of Pakistan to deliver on his promise last night to find the killers of the kidnapped journalist Daniel Pearl and "liquidate" all Islamic terror groups.

US officials are demanding to know why the search for the 38-year-old *Wall Street Journal* correspondent ended so disastrously with his captors filming Mr Pearl being decapitated.

The White House is also investigating reports that Pakistan's secret service, the ISI, tried to do a deal for the reporter's release with the British-born and educated Islamic militant, Ahmed Omar Saeed Sheikh, who is accused of masterminding last month's abduction.

President Bush is anxious not to fracture his alliance with the Pakistani leader which is crucial to the continuing war on terrorism but he wants the General to deal urgently with his country's powerful secret service and its controversial links with Islamic groups. State Department officials said last night that some ISI agents may have been involved in the kidnap.

FBI investigators in Karachi were never told that the chief suspect, Sheikh Omar, a 27-year-old former LSE student, was in ISI's custody and still in touch with his fellow kidnappers. The US is expected to ask for the extradition of Sheikh Omar to America where he could face the death penalty for his part in the reporter's murder.

President Bush took the unusual step of immediately telephoning the Pakistani leader when he was told of Mr Pearl's death. Mr Bush was in China when he was told details of the gruesome video made by Mr Pearl's murderers.

According to a Pakistani official, in the two-minute film the reporter is seen kneeling as he reads from a statement in which he says he and his parents are Jewish. He goes on to condemn the treatment of Muslims in Kashmir and Palestine. Mr Pearl appears calm but when he finishes reading, a hand appears from behind him, grabs his hair, pulling back his head. Another hand is then seen cutting his throat with a sharp-edged weapon, like a sword, and severing his head.

The camera then zooms in to show his decapitated head and his body in convulsions while a figure who cannot be identified reads a statement in Urdu demanding the release of Pakistani prisoners being held at the US base at Guantanamo Bay in Cuba.

If not, the figure threatens: "Other Americans and the Jews should be ready to face a fate like Daniel Pearl."

The video was obtained by a Pakistani-based journalist in Karachi who handed it to the US Consulate in the city where American and Pakistani officials watched it late on Thursday night.

So far Mr Pearl's body has not been found, and security chiefs say they do not know where or when he was killed.

US diplomats informed Mr Pearl's wife, Mariane, of his murder. She is seven months pregnant, and has been staying in Karachi since her husband's abduction on January 23. In a statement, she said: "The terrorists who say they killed my husband may have taken his life, but they did not take his spirit. Danny is my life. They may have taken my life, but they did not take my spirit."

Mr Bush said: "Those who would threaten Americans, those who would engage in criminal, barbaric acts, need to know that these crimes only hurt their cause and only deepen the resolve of the United States of America to rid the world of these agents of terror."

Mr Musharraf said: "This incident has enhanced our resolve and in the days to come,

Continued on page 5, col 6

US mourns, pages 4-5
Leading article, page 25
Obituary, page 41

9 770140 046862 08

Walkers flooding across the Millennium Bridge in London yesterday when it was reopened after two years of engineering work to install shock absorbers to stop it wobbling

A safe crossing? Well, that's just no fun any more

By Robin Young

LONDON'S notorious Millennium Bridge reopened to the public yesterday and, after undergoing £5 million of improvements, stayed resolutely wobble-free.

The last time the bridge was opened in June 2000 it writhed like a giant snake as thousands of people made their way across. Many thought this tremendous fun but others were left clinging to the handrails, and after a few days it was closed.

To solve the problem engineers have fitted it with 90 custom-built shock absorbers, which, much to their relief, appear to have done the trick. Yesterday strong winds were the biggest hazard faced by those crossing the £18 million bridge which links the north and south banks of the Thames near St Paul's Cathedral and the Tate Modern.

Adam Tait, from East Dulwich, who had been at the original opening and was one of the first to cross this time, said: "This is not nearly as exciting as last time. Then it was really funny." The costly modifications were road-tested in advance by 2,000 bridge walkers. The results were assessed by the consulting engineers, Arup, who had to bear much of the cost of the remedial work.

Malcolm Reading, project director for the Millennium Bridge Trust, said that the bridge was still not entirely stable. "There is still some life in it. People can feel that they are on a beautiful suspension bridge, but there is no more discomfort and certainly no need to cling on to the handrails."

Lord Foster of Thames Bank, the bridge designer, said he would jump off it if it wobbled again. "We went back to the drawing board and now we are confident the bridge will remain sturdy."

Hope for peace in Angola after Savimbi death report

From Michael Dynes in Johannesburg

HOPES for an end to the 25-year civil war in Angola were boosted yesterday after reports that Jonas Savimbi, the veteran leader of the rebel United Front for the Total Liberation of Angola (Unita), had been killed in heavy fighting with government forces.

Aldemiro Vaz da Conceicao, an Angolan presidential spokesman, was quoted on Portugal's privately-owned TSF radio station saying that Mr Savimbi's body was now in government hands, and would soon be shown to the public. Angolan government troops greeted the news by firing in the streets.

Angola's armed forces said that Mr Savimbi, 67, died during an army attack on the rebel movement's stronghold in Moxico province, in the south east of the country some 480 miles from the capital at around 3pm yesterday. There was no independent confirmation of the claim, but American diplomats in Luanda said that they were 99 per cent certain that Mr Savimbi was dead. The authorities in Luanda said that footage of his body would be broadcast on state television today.

Reports of Mr Savimbi's capture or death have occurred on numerous occasions during the conflict which has brought one of the continent's potentially richest countries to its knees. Nevertheless, there is little doubt that the string of government military victories over the past two years have brought Mr Savimbi's rebel movement to the lowest point in its history.

Angola's vast oil reserves have provided the Government of Eduardo dos Santos with the huge sums needed to prosecute the war against the rebels, while the country's immense diamond wealth has helped fund Unita's insurrection, despite UN sanctions.

In October 1999, the Luandan Government captured Mr Savimbi's military headquarters in Andulo, and took the Unita-held town of Bailundo in Angola's central highlands.

The Government's military successes in Unita's traditional heartlands came as a profound psychological blow to the rebel movement, from which it seems never to have fully recovered. Regional military analysts and diplomats say, however, that reports of Mr Savimbi's final demise should be treated with caution. Unita's leadership have proved themselves to be masters of guerrilla tactics, melting into the bush in the face of government offensives and reappearing to engage in fresh skirmishes when local observers predicted they were finished.

More than two million people have lost their homes during nearly three decades of fighting and international aid agencies are keeping another two million a year from dying from starvation.

Mr Savimbi's death, if confirmed, could be expected to break the back of the rebel movement. But military analysts gave warning that Mr Savimbi has sufficient support for a new generation of leaders to emerge to continue the war.

WHAT'S IMPORTANT

More Sport, News and Business in The Times

"Like Morse, he enjoyed classical music and poetry." Read John Thaw's obituary in The Register, **page 40**

Plus a bigger Faith page

"Ruth Ellis would never be convicted of murder now and should not have been convicted of murder then." Ben Macintyre on **page 24**

Times cartoonist Peter Brookes's award-winning Nature Notes now appears on **page 24**

Plus 13 pages of Sport

THE TIMES

Posh address for Beckham baby

By Tim Reid

THE England football captain, David Beckham, and his wife Victoria, better known as the pop singer Posh Spice, are expecting their second child in September, they announced yesterday.

The news — released in a press statement that also managed to mention the football World Cup finals and Mrs Beckham's latest Top Ten hit in the same sentence — immediately triggered fevered speculation about where the child was conceived.

Their son Brooklyn, who was born in March 1999, was said to have been named after the New York borough where he was conceived and the early money last night was on a new brother or sister in September named Knightsbridge.

Beckham, 26, who earlier this week signed a deal with Marks & Spencer to create a range of clothes for boys aged six to 14, started only one match out of eight for Manchester United between December 1 and January 6, a period in which he had much time on his hands and a weekend off on December 15 and 16. He used the opportunity to take his 27-year-old wife, a voracious purchaser of designer clothing, on a shopping spree in Knightsbridge, Central London, where they are also believed to have stayed. They were photographed in a number of exclusive shops and Mr Beckham, on his own, was seen buying a bra and G-string from the underwear store Agent Provocateur.

Their statement said: "This year has been such an exciting year for us — England are in the World Cup finals, Victoria's had a second Top Ten hit — and now we are expecting a new baby. It's fantastic.

"Brooklyn is also really looking forward to having a little brother or sister to play with."

John Glover, who recently took over management of the former Spice Girl, said: "It is wonderful news."

He added that Mrs Beckham would continue her pop career and has a new single out in May.

The stories shown on the front page are the ones thought to have the most *news value*. Newspaper editors choose stories to put on the front page that they think will make people buy the paper to find out more.

Stories are thought to have news value if they fit one or more of the characteristics shown below. If stories have several of these characteristics, newspaper editors see them as stories with great news value.

A story has news value if it:

* is dramatic

* has good pictures available

* can be told simply and quickly

* is recent

* affects a lot of people

* involves powerful or famous people

* involves 'human interest'

* is interesting to the people who usually read the paper

* is controversial – has people arguing and fighting

* is bad news

* is bizarre, amusing or quirky

Activity

Work in groups of three or four. Bring to class the front pages of two different papers, bought on the same day. Try to find a 'tabloid' newspaper, such as the *Sun*, and a 'broadsheet' newspaper, such as the *Guardian*. Use the points on the right to compare the front pages.

- How many stories does each paper cover on the front page?
- Do the two newspapers cover the same stories?
- Are there any pictures to go with the stories?
- Which stories are given most space and the biggest headlines?
- Which news value characteristics (see above left) do the stories illustrate?
- Are there any stories that have great news value?
- How would you describe the difference between the two newspapers?

5.2 Write your own radio news bulletin

Radio and television journalists are also influenced by news values. Instead of a newspaper front page, they have to fill a fixed-time news bulletin.

To write a news bulletin, journalists sort through all the information they have. This can include:

* newspaper reports
* stories dug up by their own reporters
* tips phoned in by the public
* information from the police, local councils or government departments
* press releases from different groups
* items from press agencies.

They have to decide which stories have news value, how much time each should have and what order they should follow in the bulletin. Some items are given additional time because an interview is included.

The news on the hour... Today in the Pacific Ocean a dramatic rescue took place during the Round the World yacht race. As the leading boat capsized in the fierce winds and heavy seas...

Activity

Work in groups of about three or four. Your task is to write a local radio news bulletin of *exactly* three minutes. If you can, make a tape recording of the bulletin to play back to the class. You could use a computer to help you put your bulletin together and edit it. You might be able to get help from a local journalist.

The news items that may go in your bulletin appear on pages 91–93. Remember, you have to select items, put them in order and decide how long to give each. You also have to decide which items you will not include in the bulletin.

It is worth knowing that when you write a script to be read on radio: *three words = one second (approximately) of broadcast time.*

Also, news sometimes comes into a newsroom late and has to be added at the last minute. Be ready.

Most news bulletins end on a light note with a slightly humorous item or an item of good news. This is called 'And finally...'

You now have 45 minutes to write the three-minute bulletin and be ready to record it. At the end of 45 minutes you must stop writing. In a real radio station, you would now be going on air.

Here is the first *40 seconds* of the ten o'clock news bulletin to help you. You have to write the eleven o'clock bulletin.

Music/jingle to introduce bulletin: 5 seconds

Newsreader:

Good morning. Here is the ten o'clock news from Radio Rave. This is Alex Saunders.

Police are continuing to question a man about a hold-up at Bollings Supermarket last week in which £200,000 was seized. The man, in his late twenties, was arrested yesterday evening at his home. Police say they are still looking for his female accomplice. She is also in her late twenties, about five foot three inches, and thought to be blonde.

The Prime Minister is due to visit the local hospital tomorrow. He will be thanking medical staff for their efforts following the multiple car crash just outside the town two weeks ago.

News items:

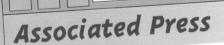

Associated Press

News is just coming in of the hijack of an aeroplane. The plane, a chartered flight returning holidaymakers from a fortnight in Spain, is owned by NiceTime Holidays Limited. The hijackers have radioed a message to Manchester Airport demanding to be allowed to land in two hours' time. It is unclear what their motives are, as yet.

Press release

The Townswomen's Guild has elected a new Treasurer who will take over her post on 1 June. Mrs Pauline Johnson takes over from Miss Alison Roberts, who is retiring to devote more time to her dogs. Mrs Johnson has had a distinguished career in accounting, having worked for world-famous accountants Addup & Spend. She said, 'I am delighted to be taking over from Miss Roberts, who has given long service to the Townswomen's Guild.'

Road crash survivors leave hospital

Three lucky survivors of the horrific road crash on the by-pass left hospital today and thanked the ambulance crew and medical staff for looking after them. Fourteen people died in the 30-vehicle pile-up which was caused by a tanker overturning in thick fog. One police officer who attended the scene said, 'In forty years of service, I have never seen such a mess. It was amazing that anyone came out alive.' James and Jenny Long, and Hamish McKinloch escaped with broken bones and bruising. However, they will spend several more months recovering at home. More survivors will be leaving the hospital later this week. The Prime Minister will visit the hospital to thank the staff personally for their efforts immediately following the crash.

Telephone message

Time taken: 9a.m.

By: Jules

A man phoned from a car on the M72. He said he had just seen a high-speed car chase involving a Porsche and two police cars in the fast lane of the motorway. The cars seemed to be doing at least 120mph. The driver of the Porsche had long blond hair. The man left his mobile number in case we want to follow this up. It is 0888545454.

Press release

Big Bargain, the supermarket chain, announce that they are opening a new store in Water Street. The first 50 customers will receive a glass of wine and a £10 shopping voucher.

From: Neema Subham nsubham@rave.co.uk
To: Duty newsdesk journalist
Sent: 15 May 08:15
Subject: Substandard housing on Finches Estate

I have been investigating the tenants' complaints about the state of repair of the flats on Finches Estate. I visited the estate and saw some of the worst properties. There really is a huge amount of damp and disrepair. The tenants' association is led by Mr Yusuf. He gave me this quote: 'We have tried and tried to get the council along to inspect the flats. They keep putting us off and saying we are not the priority estate at present. The children are becoming ill with the damp. What do we have to do to get some help here? We are law-abiding people and don't want to stop paying rent, but we can see no other way.'

I rang the council and they have no one available for comment. Do you want to cover the story on the news bulletin?

Neema

Memo

Strictly confidential

**To all shop stewards of the
General Car Workers' Union in Anytown**

Following the threats of closure of the local assembly plant, currently employing 2000 people, the union supports the workers in their threat of an immediate work-to-rule until the management agrees to negotiate. Do not release this news to the press until it has been ratified by the general council.

Radio Rave Newsdesk
The Porch
Station Road
Anytown

Dear Radio Rave,

I just want to thank you for your local news coverage, which is always very interesting and up to date. In particular, I like the way you cover national stories, and local issues and people. I would like to tell you about the firefighter who saved my cat, Mowgli, yesterday. The crew came to the rescue when my mum phoned to say the cat was stuck on the roof of our house. She's only a kitten and had been up there all night. The firefighter, Mick, went up the ladder and brought her down, but she jumped from his arms halfway down and he fell off the ladder, landing on Mowgli. She broke her leg and is now wearing a cast. He broke his leg too and had to go straight to hospital. They now have matching casts. Please mention them on your news programme.

Yours,
Sam Jones

PRESS RELEASE

Softwood School is to spend £1 million on a new sports hall and gymnasium. The money comes from a generous gift made to the school by an ex-pupil who wishes to remain anonymous. The school, which recently had a successful Ofsted inspection, has been hoping to build new sports facilities for some time. The school has produced some very successful sportsmen and sportswomen in the past and hopes the new facilities will help them to do so again. Softwood will also encourage the local community to use the facilities once they are completed.

Telephone message

Time taken: 8.30a.m.

By: Jules

A small gas explosion took place in a baker's shop in the high street. Nobody was hurt and there was little damage. A small fire was easily put out by staff.

Some news is interesting to listeners and readers, just as it is. For example, people really wanted to hear about the death of Diana, Princess of Wales and journalists found it difficult to produce enough news to satisfy them.

But sometimes there isn't much news about or it is not very interesting. It is part of the journalist's skill to make news seem interesting, even when it isn't. News is not neutral. It can be told in different ways, so that people can think the news is good or bad. You can give news a particular 'slant' or 'spin', or you can exaggerate the importance of the events.

Compare these two headlines:

Local people not too happy about proposed housing development

Fury at plans to build on local beauty spot

Which one seems more interesting and why? Which one would you use if you were a newspaper editor?

Activity

1 **Match these headlines into pairs representing the same story but with different slants.**
2 **Choose the headline from each matched pair that a news editor would probably select.**
3 **Make up some attention-grabbing newspaper headlines of your own.**

A Cliff houses set to fall into sea

B Soap actress goes into hospital for cosmetic face treatment

C New environmental report reveals that cliffs are crumbling

D **Caribbean island homes destroyed by waves**

E **Unruly schoolchildren call old lady names**

F Dog nips Vic in park

G **50-foot waves destroy homes on paradise island – dramatic pictures**

H **Vicious dog takes a chunk out of churchman**

I 'My nose nightmare!' bemoans sexy soap star

J **Yobs terrorise granny**

K **Train derailed – nobody hurt**

L **Miraculous escape for the 8.45 from Waterloo**

Be a spin doctor

It is not just journalists who influence how we feel about the news. Some people want to be in the news, but they want to appear in the best possible light. For example, political parties and governments want voters to hear about what they think and what they plan to do. They want people to think well of them, so that they will vote for their party at elections. Politicians use 'press officers' to talk to journalists and to try to make sure that the news sounds good. This is sometimes called 'spinning' the news, and the people who do it are called 'spin doctors'.

Messenger

MP says there is a silver lining

'Londoners will get much fitter now that the Underground and buses have stopped running'

Activity

1 You are going to be a spin doctor. You are going to make a story sound good. Here are two stories that might seem like bad news. Working in pairs, choose one of the stories and rewrite it to sound more positive.

2 Still in pairs, write a short 'bad news' story. Then swap your story with another pair who have to put a 'spin' on the story to make it sound better.

Compulsory homework to be introduced in primary schools

All children over the age of seven are to have one hour's compulsory homework every night, according to an announcement from the Department for Education. The homework will keep young children busy in the evenings and will also improve educational standards.

Huge tax increases to fund nurseries

The government has announced that everybody will pay more tax, amounting to around £300 each year for an average earner. Even workers on the lowest wage will pay the extra tax. The money the government gets will be used to fund an expansion in nurseries. Every baby over the age of

three months will have an automatic right to a free place in a nursery if its mother wishes to return to work.

A photograph from the feature on Sting in *Hello* magazine

Hear'Say Kym says OK! to £300,000 wedding

FORMER Hear'Say singer Kym Marsh has agreed a £300,000 deal to let celebrity gossip magazine *OK!* cover her wedding to EastEnders actor Jack Ryder. The agreement was negotiated before she announced she was quitting the band created from entrants to ITV's Popstars show. The figure puts Marsh and Ryder – who plays Jamie Mitchell in the BBC soap – in the same league as Joan Collins, who recently sold *OK!* the rights to feature her marriage to Percy Gibson. But they have failed to scale the dizzying heights reached by David and Victoria Beckham, who received £1 million for coverage of their wedding, or Michael Douglas and Catherine Zeta Jones, who were paid £2 million.

An article from *Metro* newspaper, 29 January 2002

Some people like being in the news. Celebrities need publicity to stay popular. Being in the news helps them to make more money. If they become less popular, they don't get as much work. Actors, singers, movie stars, football stars, pop groups and other celebrities need people to find them interesting – to be fans. They often have fan clubs so that people can find out more about them. This kind of publicity helps to sell CDs, posters, tickets to films and shows.

Celebrities often allow a magazine to photograph their wedding or their home in return for large sums of money.

The public are not satisfied with hearing just what the celebrity wants them to know. If they are interested in someone, they want to find out about every little bit of the star's life, even their private life – especially any scandal, involving relationships, or where crime, sex or drugs might be involved. If a famous person gets involved in a scandal, newspapers go to great lengths to get the story. Celebrities are followed around by the press in case there is an interesting story to tell about their lives.

If people feel that the press has behaved badly, they can complain to the Press Complaints Commission (PCC). This was set up to keep an eye on the press and to decide when the press has broken its Code of Practice.

The PCC uses the following headings to decide whether each complaint is justified:

Discuss

Working with a partner, look at the photos and newspaper article on the opposite page.
1 Why do you think celebrities are willing, and even keen, to let newspapers and magazines publish details about their homes and their private lives? Think about:
a) commercial (money-making) reasons
b) personal reasons, e.g. wanting people to admire their lifestyles.
2 Why do you think so many celebrities have set up their own websites?

Accuracy – reports should be accurate and an apology must be published later if not

Opportunity to reply – people must be able to reply to inaccuracies

Privacy – people have a right to privacy and the use of long-lens photography is not allowed

Harassment – journalists and photographers must not continue to telephone or question after being asked to leave

Intrusion into grief or shock – enquiries must be sensitive when people are shocked or grieving

Children – children under the age of sixteen should not be photographed or interviewed on subjects involving their welfare without an adult present. They should not be approached at school. Children involved in sex cases should not be identified

Reporting of crime – relatives and friends of people convicted should not be identified, especially children

Victims of sexual assault – victims must not be identified unless there is justification

Misrepresentation – journalists cannot use trickery (e.g. pretending to be somebody else) to get a story unless this can be justified in the public interest

Discrimination – journalists must not use a person's race, colour, religion, sex, sexual orientation or disability to describe them unless directly relevant to the story

Payment for articles – payment must not be made to witnesses in a court case or to convicted criminals for a story

Listening devices – no listening devices can be used

Hospitals – journalists and photographers must make themselves known to the authorities before entering public areas

Financial journalism – journalists must not use any information for their own gain

Confidential sources – journalists must respect confidential sources

To publish or not?

You and a partner are the editors of a newspaper. You know that your readers are interested in politicians and celebrities. The following stories and photographs have been collected by journalists. Should you publish or not?

1 Consult the PCC Code of Practice on page 97 and decide whether each story breaks the code – and whether you would publish anyway.
2 Make up one or two cases of your own (or use news stories you have heard about) to give to other pairs or to discuss in class.
3 Bring in some magazines – *Hello*, *OK!*, pop magazines – and look at the way celebrities are shown in them.

Discuss the complaints celebrities may have when their images are used in this way. Think about:
  a) intrusions into their privacy
  b) being pestered in the street by people who think they know them
  c) stalkers.

■ A woman has claimed that a famous politician told her secrets while they were having an affair. The politician denies knowing her. A photographer has photographs of the pair together. He took the pictures using a long-lens camera.

■ A celebrity has agreed that a well-known magazine can take and publish photographs of her wedding. No photographs are allowed to be taken by other newspapers or magazines. However, one of your newspaper photographers has managed to take some photographs secretly by pretending to be one of the caterers. One of your reporters also managed to interview guests by pretending to be from the rival magazine.

Royal maid reveals secret – exclusive

■ The maid of a member of the royal family has a very interesting story to tell about a relationship between the royal and a film star. She says she has also got evidence of the drunken activities of two young princesses, one of whom is under 16. There is even some talk that they may have been taking drugs.

The maid wants a lot of money for the stories.

■ A well-known football player has been involved in a drunken brawl in a nightclub. The fight was over a girl that the footballer has been seeing. However, he is married with children and does not want the story to be made public. Your reporter has collected interviews from people who know the footballer and she wants to get photographs of the footballer with his family outside his house.

The footballer is angry. He says it is his private life and has nothing to do with anybody else. He says he is going to complain to the Press Council.

5.5 How free should the press be?

In a democratic country, the press fulfils a very important role by revealing information about the mistakes and wrongdoings of people in powerful positions. This is why some governments try to control the press – they don't want people to read news stories that show them or their actions in a bad light. Journalists see themselves as helping to keep people informed by telling them the truth, even if sometimes this means revealing private details. A free press is essential in a democratic society.

However, there is another side to it. Some journalists pry into the lives of people so much that they cause upset and anger. They want to get the 'dirt' on somebody, no matter what damage this causes. These journalists say that this is fair for people like celebrities and politicians who seek publicity.

Libel

What can people do if they think the press has gone too far or is telling lies about their private life?

People can sue newspapers or television companies for libel. If they can prove that the reports are lies then the court can order the newspapers or TV companies to pay huge sums of money.

Some very rich and powerful people have used the threat of libel to stop newspapers printing stories about them. The newspapers were frightened to get into expensive court cases even though they believed their stories to be true.

Activity

1 What does the word 'libel' mean?
2 Read case study 1. How did Jonathan Aitken use the law of libel to try to prevent the truth about him coming out?
3 Why do you think it is important that journalists investigate politicians to find out if they are corrupt or telling lies?
4 What happens in countries where the government can censor the press and stop journalists writing stories about politicians?

Case study 1: Jonathan Aitken

Jonathan Aitken was a Cabinet minister who was accused of using his position in the government to make money out of arms deals with Saudi Arabia. He had close personal and business dealings with two Saudi princes who paid for him to stay at the Ritz, a luxury hotel in Paris, in 1993. The *Guardian* newspaper found out about this and started to enquire into his affairs. Aitken denied that the Saudi princes had paid his hotel bill. In 1995, Aitken sued the *Guardian* for libel to stop it publishing stories about him. He was hoping to frighten it off. But the *Guardian* went ahead and in the resulting court case Aitken was found to be lying. He was later charged with perjury (lying in court) and sent to prison.

Just before the court case, Aitken used these famous words: 'If it falls to me to start a fight to cut out the cancer of bent and twisted journalism in our country with the simple sword of truth and the trusty shield of fair play, so be it.'

Case study 2: Naomi Campbell

A source close to Naomi was quoted as saying:

She wants to clean up her life for good. She went into modelling when she was very young and it is easy to get led astray. Drink and drugs were unfortunately widely available in the fashion world. But Naomi has realised that she has a problem and has bravely vowed to do something about it.

Naomi Campbell said:

When someone is having medical treatment, they should have the right to privacy.

Comments by Piers Morgan, the editor of the *Daily Mirror*:

It [drug taking] is against the law and when someone, a role model, breaks the law, the press has a duty to expose them.

She is one of the most shameless self-publicists in celebrity history.

Kylie Minogue said:

You can't be in this business and expect people to give you all the attention you want when you want it but not when you don't want it. I've always been of the opinion you have to take the good with the bad.

The *Daily Mirror* published a photograph of Naomi Campbell leaving a Narcotics Anonymous meeting in the King's Road, London, in what the paper described as 'a courageous bid to beat her addiction to drink and drugs'. The paper went on to say that she had been having regular counselling sessions for three months. Naomi decided that the paper had gone too far into her private life and revealed something she did not want the public to know about. She sued the *Daily Mirror* for 'unlawful invasion of privacy'.

The *Daily Mirror* claimed that:

* it treated her case sympathetically
* people at the meeting knew who she was
* when speaking publicly about drugs, Campbell had said she had never taken them.

Naomi won the case but was only awarded £3,500 damages, an almost insignificant amount. The judge said she lied in court and was 'misleading' and 'manipulative'.

Activity

1 **What do you think about the Naomi Campbell case?**
   a) **Was it fair for the *Daily Mirror* to publish her photograph and stories about her drug addiction?**
   b) **Should Campbell be entitled to privacy when she often uses the press to promote herself and things she sells, e.g. her range of perfume?**
2 **Do celebrities like Campbell have a right to complain when newspapers and magazines print stories about their private lives?**
3 **Would you bring in a new 'privacy' law to control the freedom of the press in this area? Explain why or why not. If you say yes, what might the law say?**

In the public interest?

The issue of press freedom is often a balance between privacy and public interest. People have a right to privacy, but there is sometimes a public interest in revealing what people do in private. The problem is that it can be very difficult to decide exactly what 'public interest' means. It does not simply mean that the public are interested. The public – the readers of newspapers and watchers of television – are interested in most things about people, particularly their relationships and their sex lives.

'Public interest' is when it is important to know something about someone because they are public figures or because what they do affects other people. For instance, if a member of the government accepts money or holidays from a rich businessman and then helps the man win a government building contract worth £2 million, then we should know. If a surgeon is taking drugs and attending wild parties while people are dying under her care, then we should know.

But how far should the press go? When do we have the right to know about the private life of a politician or celebrity, if at all? And what about their families? Sometimes the distinction between stories that are in the public interest and those that are not is a very fine one. For example: a news story that a politician's wife recently had an abortion is not in the public interest; there is no reason why we should know this. However, if the politician is an active anti-abortion campaigner, then it could be in the public interest and maybe we should know.

1 Working in pairs or threes, examine the fictitious cases opposite. Decide whether or not each story is in the public interest.

2 Now redo this activity, but in each case read the additional information printed upside-down at the bottom of this page. See if this makes you change your mind. In some cases it might; in others it won't.

---

1 It is not certain that the child is his, although he is known to have spent time with the actress.

2 The politician has the power to award business contracts licensing UK companies to sell arms to Middle Eastern countries. He wants Britain to have a good relationship with these countries so that they will buy arms from Britain.

3 The presenter has never made any statements about weight or about being thin or fat.

4 He has been having an affair with his secretary and they intend to marry.

5 The businessman claims that the stories are not true and that they will ruin his business if they come out.

6 The MP says that it is not true and that the story is damaging his reputation.

7 The actress had previously appeared naked in a film.

8 The tobacco companies say that it is not their policy to encourage children to smoke. They say that they advertise to encourage existing smokers to buy particular brands.

1

There is a story that a male member of the royal family has had an illegitimate child with a film actress.

2

A government politician has been taking very expensive holidays in a number of Middle Eastern countries, staying in the best hotels and on the yachts of rich Middle Eastern businessmen and politicians.

3

A television presenter is shown in photographs to have put on a considerable amount of weight. Newspapers show her with captions such as 'Presenter breaks the scales' and 'Presenter fills the screen'.

4

The Foreign Secretary is divorcing his wife. The wife is very bitter and wants to talk to the press. There have been a number of stories in the press, and everywhere the Foreign Secretary goes he is asked questions about it. It is interfering in his work.

5

It is rumoured that a very powerful businessman has been using money from the pension fund that belongs to his workers. He is using it to do deals to rescue his failing business. The businessman has tried to stop newspapers printing stories by threatening to sue them for libel.

6

A Member of Parliament is receiving money from a wealthy foreign businessman to help him get a British passport. He is also doing favours for the businessman by providing him with information.

7

A well-known actress is caught sunbathing on a Caribbean island without her bikini top. The next day photographs of her topless are on the front pages of several newspapers. She is furious.

8

It is reported that tobacco companies are deliberately targeting young people in developing countries to try to encourage them to smoke cigarettes.

Press

This includes newspapers and magazines. Newspapers are daily or weekly. They can be grouped into:

* tabloids – smaller papers like the *Sun* and the *Mirror*, which are easier to read but do not provide so much news or detailed analysis. They usually have wide coverage of sport and stories relating to TV personalities or celebrities
* broadsheets – larger papers like *The Times* and the *Guardian*, which contain more serious news stories and coverage of world events.

Daily paper	Circulation (000)
Sun	3,519
Daily Mail	2,464
Mirror	2,222
Daily Telegraph	1,009
Daily Express	959
The Times	701
Financial Times	462
Evening Standard	418
Guardian	397
Independent	223
Scotsman	85
Racing Post	77

Sunday paper	Circulation (000)
News of the World	4,051
Mail on Sunday	2,407
Sunday Mirror	1,869
Sunday People	1,401
The Sunday Times	1,316
Sunday Express	888
Sunday Telegraph	787
Sunday Mail	702
Observer	461
Independent on Sunday	234
Sunday Sport	196
Scotland on Sunday	87
Sunday Business	55

Circulation figures for October 2001

There are a huge number of different magazines. They tend to come out weekly or monthly.

The Press Complaints Commission makes sure that newspapers and magazines follow a code of practice (see page 97). This says they should not publish inaccurate or misleading stories. They should also respect an individual's privacy (unless there is a 'public interest' in something the individual has done) and not harass people. The Commission also looks into complaints.

Television

There are terrestrial channels like the BBC and ITV (independent television) and satellite channels like Sky. Television can also be provided by way of cables. The newest development is digital television, which allows viewers to receive many more channels on their TV sets.

The BBC has regulations to control its standards. It says its programmes should be accurate, truthful, balanced and fair to the people who take part. Independent television is regulated by the Independent Television Commission (ITC). It looks after viewers' interests by setting standards for programmes and advertising.

The internet

The internet is a source of information on a limitless number of topics. It is also used increasingly to sell goods and services to users. Messages can be sent by e-mail. The internet is not regulated, although users can employ devices to limit the parts of the internet coming into their personal computer.

Advertising

Advertisements can be found in a variety of forms on TV, radio, in the cinema, on posters, at sports events and in many other places.

The Advertising Standards Authority was set up in 1962 to make sure that advertisements in the UK are legal, decent and truthful. It handles complaints and can insist that adverts are withdrawn immediately.

section 6
Global citizenship
Can you change the world?

Key words
- child labour
- environmental impact
- fair trade
- tourism

We are global citizens. Every time we go to the shops, we buy things produced or made abroad. The prices we pay for things depend on world markets. Jobs in our own town may be provided by foreign companies. People are likely to work for companies with offices abroad, and they may be expected to move abroad to live and to work. International agreements and European laws directly affect us. Increasingly, people travel abroad for their holidays and many are travelling to faraway places like Australia and Thailand.

We are affected by global issues. We hear daily news of other countries. Sometimes this is news of wars or disasters, like famine and floods. We give money to charities to help people in difficulties. British soldiers and aid workers go to countries around the world. Events in other parts of the world can affect our lives directly. If a foreign company is in difficulties, factories in Britain employing thousands of workers may close. Global warming affects weather in the UK just as it does in other countries.

We also have an influence on people in other countries. What we buy, where we go and how we behave can help other people or make their lives worse. If we buy goods made by child workers, what does this mean for them? If we expect to pay very little for chocolate, who suffers? What happens to neighbouring countries when we create waste or pollution? How does our foreign holiday affect the people who live in the country we go to?

All this means that we need to think about our role in the world and what kind of a world we would like it to be.

In this section you will learn about:

* international trade and how it affects workers in other countries
* child labour
* the impact of tourism
* the role of the European Union.

You will:

* analyse information
* form opinions and justify them
* take part in group discussions
* think about and explain views that are not your own
* think about other people's experiences.

6.1 How can trade be made fairer?

Trade is one of the most important ways in which we have contact with other countries. If you look in your kitchen cupboard, you will find food products and drinks that use raw materials from all over the world. But many farmers in the developing world have problems that we never think about when we peel a banana, eat a bar of chocolate or drink a cup of tea.

Our pay is so low, my sons have gone to the hills to grow marijuana for more money – but they are breaking the law.

Women in the banana packing sheds suffer double the normal rate of leukaemia. Many babies are born deformed.

Windward Islands (bananas)

Pesticides sprayed on the bananas can have terrible side effects – they can make men sterile.

One hurricane, or volcanic eruption, can ruin all the banana trees – then we've lost everything.

Colombia (coffee)

Our coffee beans can change hands 150 times before they reach you, the consumer. We only get a tiny amount of the price you pay.

With coffee prices so low, many of us have been forced to leave our land and move to the cities to find work.

Activity

Use the information on these two pages to investigate some of the difficulties faced by farmers in the developing world.

1 What sorts of problems do they have?

Northern India (tea)

When the parents earn very little, the children have to work too. This means they don't go to school.

Our houses are in a terrible condition, but if we complain to the estate manager we risk losing our jobs. Any shelter is better than none.

Ghana (cocoa)

When cocoa prices fall, we have to make difficult decisions. We may have to put off sending our children to school, and we can only buy medicines for members of the family who have work.

It's not just the people who get ill – capsids and mealy bugs can destroy 25–30 per cent of the cocoa crop each year, if we're not able to look after the plants properly.

2 **Put these problems into two groups:**
   - **problems to do with the natural world**
   - **problems to do with other people.**

3 **How could farmers overcome some of these problems?**

Can trade be fair?

In the developing world many farmers who grow products such as tea, coffee, cocoa and bananas are poor and getting poorer. They have to sell their crop to traders who pay very little, and the money they earn is often less than the cost of harvesting the crop. They can only borrow money at very high interest rates and they live in constant debt. They can't afford to send their children to school or improve their homes. Farmers who work on plantations owned by large companies have further problems, such as unsafe working conditions and poor, basic housing. They cannot join a union or take any part in decisions that affect their life on the plantation.

The case study below shows that something can be done to help these farmers.

I'm Christina Peck. We live in a small, simple cabin in Belize, Central America. Our home is basic – we have no electricity, or indoor water supply. We are cocoa farmers. It's hard work. The crops have to be carefully tended; then, once the cocoa pods have been picked, the beans have to be dried. Justino has to carry a 45 kg sack of beans on his back, across two miles of rough roads. Then he has a two-hour bus journey to the warehouse, where the beans are stored before being shipped to Europe, where they're made into chocolate for you to eat.

Case study: the Peck family

Chocolate is made from cocoa beans, which only grow where there is a hot climate. Two-thirds of the world's cocoa is grown by 'smallholders' – individual farmers who work for themselves. The Peck family tell their story:

I'm Justino. About ten years ago we were managing on the money we earned from selling cocoa beans. We could buy the basic things we needed. Then, suddenly, the price of cocoa fell, and our beans were only worth half what they had been. We had no money to buy food and clothes – things were desperate for us and our neighbours. We got together and set up a co-operative. This meant we could work together to transport and market our cocoa, keeping our costs down. But we had to borrow money to do this and it became more and more difficult to repay our debts. Some of our neighbours had no choice but to give up, leave their land and look for work on plantations or in the city.

Then, out of the blue, we were approached by Green and Black's, the UK chocolate company, who wanted to buy our cocoa! They offered us a much higher price for our beans, and guaranteed to pay it for three years, buying all the cocoa we could produce. They used our cocoa to make 'Maya Gold' chocolate, the first brand to be given the Fairtrade Mark. Now life is much better. Farmers have returned to their villages to grow cocoa. Communities are back together again.

We've used some of the money to make a concrete floor in our house – before we just had a dirt floor. We can now afford to send our children to secondary school, as well as buying them schoolbooks and shoes. We've planted more cocoa, because of our confidence in fair trade – it really does make a difference.

Activity

What do you think about the way the UK trades with other countries?

1   **Read the statements below. Arrange them according to how strongly you agree, or disagree with them. When you have finished, have a class discussion to see if everybody feels the same way.**

A If farmers in the developing world had fewer children, and worked harder, they'd be better off.

B If we buy fair trade products, we can make a difference to the lives of thousands of farmers in the developing world.

C Farmers in the UK deserve more support than farmers on the other side of the world.

D Supermarkets in the UK should provide the consumer with food at the lowest possible prices.

E Multinational companies which control much of the world's trade are a good thing – they provide jobs for thousands of people in rich and poor

G The UK should import less food from countries where people don't have enough to eat.

F The main thing to change is us – we should be prepared to pay a little more for fair trade products.

I It's up to the governments of developing countries to help their poor, not up to UK consumers.

H Fair trade foods taste just as good, or better, than other brands.

2   **Look at this diagram. Who should be responsible for making trade fair?**

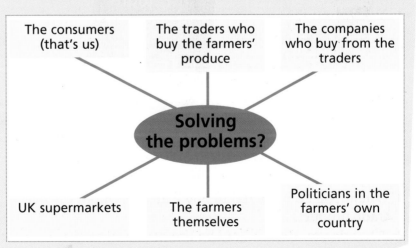

The consumers (that's us)   The traders who buy the farmers' produce   The companies who buy from the traders

Solving the problems?

UK supermarkets   The farmers themselves   Politicians in the farmers' own country

What is fair trade?

* **Fair trade** means paying farmers in the developing world a fair price for what they produce. This means that they can have more control over their lives, and improve their standard of living.

* **The Fairtrade Mark** is a consumer label. Look for it on products in your supermarket. It guarantees that the farmers who produced the food originally were paid a fair price.

* **The Fairtrade Foundation** awards the Fairtrade Mark to products that meet agreed criteria (or standards) – in other words, products that really are fairly traded.

Fair trade criteria

In order for a product to carry the Fairtrade Mark, the following conditions must be met:

1 The price paid for the product covers the cost of production.
2 Workers on plantations have decent wages, housing, and health and safety standards.
3 No child labour or forced labour is allowed.
4 A percentage of the money they earn is used by the producers to improve their living and working conditions.
5 Producers are treating the environment in a sustainable way.
6 Small-scale farmers and workers on plantations can join organisations that will help and support them, e.g. co-operatives or trade unions.
7 Contracts make sure there is long-term planning for sustainable development.
8 Advance payment is made so that smaller producers won't fall into debt.

Activity

1 Do you think the Fairtrade Mark is a good idea?
2 Would you be prepared to pay a little bit more for fair trade products?
3 What do you think would be the best way to get supermarkets to stock fair trade products?

6.2 Trade Trap – a fair trade game

You are a poor farmer in a developing country. Each year you sell your crop to traders, who sell it on to a big multinational company. Play the game and find out what life is like for you and your family.

If you're lucky, you could be selling in the fair trade market, and you'll see what difference this makes to your quality of life.

How to play

- Play in groups of four to six. Everyone will need a counter. You will need a dice (or two, if you are going to use the game cards on pages 114–115).
- Before you start, everyone needs to draw up a **money chart** (see below). You already have $100 from selling your last crop. Use the *Cost of living* tables to help you decide how to spend it.
- Put your counters on **start**, and throw the dice in turn. Whoever has the lowest score moves forward first, following the outer 'world trade' track.
- Take turns, making sure that any instructions on the squares are followed carefully. If you land on **world trade** or **fair trade chance**, pick up a chance card from the correct pile.
- Every round of the board represents one year. As you pass **trade**, pick up a trade card to find out how much money you get for that year's crop.
- Decide how to spend your money each year. You may have debts to pay and some difficult decisions to make. Keep a full record on your **money chart**.

- At the end of the game, see who is in the best situation – consider money and quality of life.

When you've played for several 'years', think about ways of developing the game. You could:

- alter the rules
- adapt the costs
- add more chance cards
- fill in other squares on the board
- change some of the trade cards.

Cost of living

These costs are for your whole family, for one year.

Essential items

These *must* be paid for each year, because it's hard to survive without them. If you can't afford them, you'll have to borrow money.

Basic housing	$10
Basic food	$50
Basic clothes	$30

Desirable items

You'll have to decide what you can afford each year – try to provide all these things for your family if you possibly can:

School	$30
School books	$10
Shoes	$10
More food or clothes	$25
Home improvements	$15

Money chart

Year	Money received	Items bought (cost)	Total spent	Money owed	Balance	Comment
1	$100					

TRADE	←	Waiting for a trader. Throw an even number to continue	←	Move on 4 squares	Contaminated water – everyone is ill. Miss a turn
↓	TRADE CARDS		Move back 1 square	→	→
↓	↱	→	FAIR TRADE CHANCE		
↓	Move on 3 squares				
↓	↑				
Fiesta! All work stops to celebrate. Miss a turn	↑				
↓	Crop needs extra weeding. Throw an even number to continue		You can only move on to the fair trade track if you pick up a chance card that says you can do so		
↓	FAIR TRADE	←	←	←	←
Trader returns and buys surplus crop. Receive $20	START	WORLD TRADE	→	Tropical storm damages crop. Throw an odd number to continue	→

FRUIT PASSION
FAIR TRADE JUICE
Fairer to Everyone

Pure ORANGE JUICE
FC 0359I

Traidcraft
GEOBAR
FOR A WHOLE WORLD OF FAIR TRADE
AN APPLE AND RAISIN SNACK BAR

APPLE   HONEY   RAISINS   OATS

LOW IN SATURATED FAT
NO ARTIFICIAL COLOURING

94% FAT FREE
6 Bars

Move back 5 squares

← ← Mysterious fungus attacks crop. Pay $5 for herbicide ←

WORLD TRADE CHANCE

→ Repairs to road needed after heavy rain. Miss a turn → →

FAIR TRADE CHANCE

Move back 4 squares

Unexpected drought: work on village well. Miss a turn

↓

Move back 2 squares

↑

CHANCE CARDS FOR FAIR TRADE

↓

↑

↓

Sick child. Pay $5 for medicine or miss a turn

TRADE Receive $130

← Fair trade company offers you a bonus for extra crop. Receive $150 when you trade

↑

Fiesta! All work stops to celebrate. Miss a turn ↩

CHANCE CARDS FOR WORLD TRADE

↑

→ → Move on 3 squares → →

WORLD TRADE CHANCE

Game cards

You can get a copy of these cards from your teacher to make sets of your own. Place each set face down on the board. Take one card each time a player trades or lands on chance, and then replace the card at the bottom of the pile. Alternatively, you can throw two dice to see what card you get. The dice numbers are in brackets on the card.

Trade cards

World price rise! Your crop is worth 20 per cent more than you were expecting — receive $120.

(2)

Trader cash crisis! Your trader has no cash to pay you. Instead he gives you basic food and clothes — receive no cash.

(3)

Your trader's scales are 'fixed'. Your crop weighs 10 per cent less than you expected it to — receive only $90.

(4)

The world price for your crop has fallen. It's only worth half what you had expected — receive $50.

(5)

Serious crop failure in another part of the world means there's a shortage of the crop you grow. It's worth more this year! Receive $110.

(6)

A bumper harvest means there's a 'glut' of your crop on the world market. Your trader only offers you $80 — take it or leave it!

(7)

Your usual trader doesn't come to your village this year. A new 'middleman' appears. You are desperate for money to live on, so have to accept the $70 he offers you.

(8)

A month ago, pests attacked your crop. Half of it was ruined. The trader will only give you $60.

(9)

The trader says he is not impressed by the quality of your crop this year. He says it's below standard. He offers you $90 — take it or leave it!

(10)

Receive $100.

(11)

If you throw 12, throw again.

(12)

Chance cards for world trade (For farmers on the world trade track)

Your roof is leaking badly. Miss a turn to fix it.

(2 or 3)

Your son needs to start secondary school. It will cost you $50 all together – he must have books and shoes for the long walk. You can borrow the money, but will have to pay back $55 when you next trade. (4 or 5)

The government has introduced a new land tax. Pay $5 now. (If you have to borrow the money, pay back $6 when you next trade.)

(6)

Fantastic news! A fair trade company says it will buy the entire crop you and your neighbours produce (as long as you agree to certain conditions). You can move on to the fair trade track next time you reach start. (7, 8 or 9)

Your mother is ill. Walk with her to the hospital (a two-day round trip – miss a go), or pay $2 for a taxi.

(10)

Rats have got into your food store. You need to buy more basic food – cost $10. (If you borrow the money, pay back $11 next time you trade.)

(11)

Your neighbours suggest you join their new co-operative. You must pay $5 now, but the tools you can share mean your crop will be better – you will earn an extra $15 when you next trade.

(12)

Chance cards for fair trade
(For farmers on the fair trade track)

A new fair trade agreement means you will earn an extra $30 when you next trade.

(2)

You can no longer use weedkillers on your crop – miss a turn to do weeding.

(3 or 4)

Your children are all ill. Pay $10 for medical care. You can borrow this until you next trade if you need to.

(5)

Thanks to fair trade, you now have a regular water supply to the village. This means less time collecting water and more time to tend your crop – you produce more. Receive an extra $20 when you next trade. (6)

You are no longer able to meet the fair trade conditions for growing your crop. Return to start and the 'world trade' track now.

(7 or 8)

You offer to help build a new medical centre – throw 2, 4 or 6 to continue.

(9)

Your co-operative can now afford to build its own school. It will only cost you $20 to send your children there.

(10)

If you throw 11 or 12, throw again.

(11 or 12)

Do they meet the Fairtrade Mark?

Work in groups of four or five. You work for the Fairtrade Foundation. You decide whether products should be awarded the Fairtrade Mark. It is your job to support poor farmers. But remember that the Fairtrade Mark guarantees to consumers that they are buying products that are genuinely fairly traded. You must make sure each product 'meets the Mark' before it's allowed to carry it.

Today your team has four different products to consider. Which of the actions in the diagram will you recommend for each product?

Yes
The product should be awarded the Fairtrade Mark without delay

Maybe
It could be awarded the Fairtrade Mark now, but with conditions set for further development, e.g. a year to cut down on use of chemicals

Perhaps
It could be awarded the Fairtrade Mark in the future, e.g. on condition that health and safety standards are improved

No
It should not be awarded the Fairtrade Mark. You have serious concerns about whether it could ever be considered 'fair trade'

1 Make sure the team understands the fair trade criteria (look back to page 110). Remember that it may be impossible for producers to meet all the criteria from the start – you may have to help them to develop and change the way they work.
2 To help you decide whether each product should carry the Fairtrade Mark, give it a score out of ten against each of the criteria. Use a chart like the one below. For criteria not mentioned in the product description score zero.
3 Decide what action you will recommend for each product.
4 When you have finished, you'll need to give a short presentation to explain your decision. You can also make recommendations to the organisations involved, if you have set certain conditions for the Mark to be awarded.

Fairtrade Mark criteria	Tea	Orange juice	Brazil nuts	Sugar
• Price covers production costs • Decent wages • Decent housing • Health and safety standards enforced • No child or forced labour • Some money reinvested to improve conditions • Environment treated with care • Union membership allowed • Long term plans for improvement • Advance payments				
Total score for each product				
Recommendation				

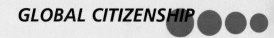

Products for your committee to discuss

Product: Tea

Producer information: We run a small tea estate in an isolated region in northern India, producing some of the most delicious tea in the world. The harsh environment here means we have to use chemicals on our crop. We do have protective clothing for the tea pickers, but most of them choose not to wear it because it's so hot. If a worker is absent after an accident at work, we have agreed to pay up to three days' wages. We cannot afford to pay our workers very much, but we will employ their families if they want them to work. Just over 30 per cent of the tea pickers' children aged from six to twelve go to school on the estate. We provide housing for our workers, made of bamboo, mud and thatch. They do not have electricity or piped water.

Product: Orange juice

Producer information: We are a group of fruit farmers in Cuba. We grow oranges and sell them to a company that processes them into orange juice. Our orange trees are carefully tended, and we are trying to use fewer pesticides or other chemicals that might harm the environment. We have set up a system to share transport costs and equipment. At the moment this is all we are able to do to help our farmers, but with a fair-trade premium for our crop, we could do more for our members. We want to help build a new medical centre and a school for all our children to attend. We also hope to have an adult education programme, which would help the farmers learn more about efficient farming methods.

Product: Brazil nuts

Producer information: We are a small trading company in Peru. We buy Brazil nuts from groups of families living in the Amazon rainforest. They gather the wild Brazil nuts, which are organic – nobody interferes with the trees in any way. When the ripe nut pods fall, the families collect them and carry them on their backs to the river. We meet the families there, and pay them a fair price for people in this area. They have no production costs. We are helping them to use the forest in a sustainable way, which means they are not cutting it down for farming. The pods go by boat to the shelling and drying factory in the nearest town. Then they are flown to Lima, sorted, graded and vacuum-packed, ready for export to Europe.

Product: Sugar

Producer information: We are a co-operative in the Philippines. We grow and mill our own sugar. Our members receive five to ten per cent more pay than other local workers. We elect a committee to make decisions about issues like health and safety. We are gradually improving our homes and all our children now go to school – if any parents are finding it hard to manage, we help with the costs of school books and uniforms. We encourage organic farming, and do not use harmful chemicals on our crops. We also have a training programme for our farmers, and we encourage the women in our community to develop their own businesses – some are raising livestock, and others produce craft items to sell in the local town.

6.3 Hard labour!

We like to buy goods like trainers, t-shirts and footballs as cheaply as we can. It means we have more money to spend on other things. But sometimes these goods have been made by people, including children or teenagers, working as 'sweated labour'. This means that the work has been done by people working for very low wages, usually in terrible conditions. Children as young as five work long hours to make the goods we want to buy. Some of these goods are not particularly cheap, so the company selling them is making a lot of profit that is not getting to the people who make them.

Activity

As you read the case studies, list the ways that the lives of the children are affected by their work.

Facts and figures

It is not possible to give accurate numbers of child labourers, because there are no official records. But it is estimated that at least 250 million children aged from five to fourteen are involved, and this figure may be as high as 500 million if child domestic work is taken into account. The highest number of child labourers are in Asia and Africa, but there are also many in richer industrialised countries. In the USA, thousands of migrant children, such as Mexican Americans, are involved in harvesting crops.

Case study 1: Sonia

Many of the footballs that people in the UK play with might well have come from India. Britain imports a lot of sports goods from the Indian subcontinent. Children are used to make them very cheaply.

Sonia is eleven years old and stitches soccer balls. She lives in a village near Jalandhar in India's Punjab. She is blind – she lost her sight at the age of seven. 'It went completely dark in front of my eyes and I was scared,' she said. 'I didn't know what was happening.' But she has learned to stitch soccer balls by touch alone – her Aunt Satya matches up the panels and passes them to her niece. The two of them are the main breadwinners for the extended family since Sonia's mother fell seriously ill. 'There's no fun in it, but I have no choice,' says Sonia, who earns seven rupees for each of the two balls she stitches in a day – not even enough to buy a litre of milk.

Adapted from the *New Internationalist*

Case study 2: Vinod

People buy 'ethnic' carpets from Pakistan, Nepal and India to put on the floors of their comfortable homes. Children are used in their manufacture because they have small hands and nimble fingers so they can tie the knots more easily. But they are also very cheap to employ and do not complain when they work in terrible conditions, often in carpet sheds, sometimes for twelve to sixteen hours a day. Often these long hours lead to illness, and sitting in cramped positions for so long can lead to malformed bones. Meanwhile these child labourers miss out on their education and have fewer chances for a good job later on.

Ten-year-old Vinod is from Dariyen village in the Indian state of Uttar Pradesh. He worked for two years for a carpet weaver. After his father's

What can we do about it?

We are global consumers – we buy goods from all over the world. If enough people get together they can influence the companies that sell the goods in our shops. But is it anything to do with us? Is it a problem that governments in other countries should sort out? What should a global citizen do?

Discuss

People respond in a variety of ways to the problem of child labour.

Discuss the statements below with a partner. Which do you agree with, disagree with, can't decide about? What do *you* think should be done?

> It's simple. If the goods are made by children, then we stop buying them. We should boycott [refuse to buy] the goods now. Then the companies will stop employing children.

> It is nothing to do with us. If the goods are cheap, buy them. We don't know about what's going on in other countries.

> We should write to our MPs to make our government put pressure on the governments of the other countries to stop child labour being used. We could put trade sanctions on the countries or refuse to give them aid (food and medicines) if child labourers continue to be used.

> We should give the companies a year or two to stop using children and replace them with adults. If they don't, we should boycott all their products.

> It is really up to the governments of the countries where the children are used as cheap labour. If they are not worried about it, then why should we be?

> We should let the children work if they want to, but make sure they work in good conditions and receive fair pay, and have some leisure time and education. We must put pressure on the companies to do this by having campaigns in this country and demonstrating and protesting outside shops which sell the goods.

> Demonstrating and protesting do not achieve anything. We are powerless to influence big multinational companies.

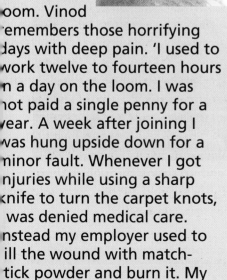

premature death, Vinod was taken by his mother to work on a loom. Vinod remembers those horrifying days with deep pain. 'I used to work twelve to fourteen hours in a day on the loom. I was not paid a single penny for a year. A week after joining I was hung upside down for a minor fault. Whenever I got injuries while using a sharp knife to turn the carpet knots, I was denied medical care. Instead my employer used to fill the wound with match-stick powder and burn it. My flesh and skin used to burn.'

Activity

Solving problems like child labour is not always straightforward. The actions we take can have consequences that we did not intend.

1 Look at the speech bubbles below. Compare what the child labourers might say with your answers and discussions from pages 118–119. What do you think now?
2 Consider some of the alternatives to factory child labour shown in the diagram at the foot of the page? Do you think these are better or worse than being a child labourer?

What might the child labourers say?

It would help us if people in your country put some pressure on the companies who employ us to stop the worst types of exploitation.

In my country you have to pay for education. My parents can't afford to pay for me – I have to earn some money so that I can be educated and get a better job in the future.

We children must be able to work. If I don't work, then I don't earn money and my family will go hungry or we won't be able to buy clothes and shoes.

I would like pressure to be put on the government of my country to make sure we have better conditions at work, shorter hours and better pay so we can have a better life.

– become a street child

– go back to doing backbreaking agricultural work

– end up sifting through rubbish for anything of value

What might happen if the children lost their jobs?

– be forced to leave home

– become involved in the child sex market

The working children's conference

The children who are worst treated will probably never have a chance to complain. But young adults and working children in different countries have started movements to try to improve their conditions of work. In November 1996, child delegates from 33 countries went to a conference in Kanapur, India. They came up with ten demands:

1 We want recognition of our problems, our proposals and our organisations.
2 We are against the boycott of products made by children.
3 We want respect and security for ourselves and the work we do.
4 We want an education system and teaching methods suited to the reality of our lives.
5 We want professional training suited to our needs and capabilities.
6 We want access to good healthcare.
7 We want to be consulted on all decisions affecting us, at local, national and international level.
8 We want the root causes of our situation, primarily poverty, to be tackled.
9 We want more activity in rural areas, so that children do not have to migrate to the cities.
10 We are against exploitation at work but we are for work with dignity, with hours adapted so that we have time for education and leisure.

Big companies are affected by public pressure. They do not like bad publicity about their products or the threat that consumers will not buy their goods. As a result, some companies now insist that children below a certain age do not work in their factories. Some invest in the areas where children work and contribute to their education. Some have put in place other schemes, e.g. healthcare and better housing. But there is a long way to go and there are still many rich companies using cheap labour in developing countries.

Companies do not like people protesting outside their shops about the child labour used to produce their products.

Activity

1 Have your views about what you should do about child labour changed after reading this material?
2 Global citizens can have an effect. Design a poster or leaflet telling people about child labour and suggesting how we can help to improve the lives of the child labourers.

6.4 How does tourism affect people in other countries?

Many people like to travel abroad for their holidays. They are not just looking for the sun and beaches. They enjoy visiting other countries where the language, food, music, buildings, history and customs are all different from home. Tourism has become the single biggest industry on Earth. It creates enormous incomes for some countries, and many people now depend on tourism for their jobs and livelihoods.

Activity

What do tourists want from a holiday? With a partner, look at the pictures on these two pages and decide the six most important things a country needs if it wants a successful holiday industry. List them in order of importance.

Entertainment – music venues, theatres

Swimming pools

Workers (for hotels, restaurants, etc.)

Historic buildings and sites

Restaurants and cafés

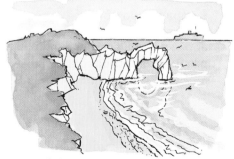

Beautiful scenery

Transport – coaches, cars for hire, trains, taxis

Nightclubs

Airport

Shops and markets

Bars

Foreign-language speakers (guides etc.)

Hotels, apartments and villas

Beaches and watersports

Museums and art galleries

The benefits and costs of tourism

Most countries that are now popular with tourists did not plan their tourism industry. It developed because people offered holidays and tourists wanted to visit.

Many aspects of a country are affected by tourism. While it can brings benefits, it can also bring problems – some of which might not have been expected.

A   Tourists cause litter and dirt. We have to spend money cleaning up after them.

B   The hotels and restaurants we build for tourists provide jobs for hundreds of people – waiters, kitchen staff, cleaners, porters, bar staff, reception staff.

C   Tourism means extra traffic. The aeroplanes, coaches, cars and taxis cause noise and pollution, which makes the air unhealthy for our children to breathe.

D   Tourism brings extra money to our country, which the government can spend on things like healthcare and schools.

E   The scenery is ruined when land is used to build hotels, apartment blocks and nightclubs.

F   Tourists don't respect our customs. People dress on the beach and in the street in a way that we find offensive.

G   Our ancient sites are being ruined by thousands of people walking on them, even vandalising them.

H Because of tourism, the government has provided more art galleries and museums for everyone to enjoy.

Your country sure is beautiful.

I Local people who want jobs in the tourist industry are willing to learn foreign languages and new skills.

J Young people get dissatisfied with their lives when they see how much money the foreign tourists have.

K We have terrible water shortages because of the swimming pools built for tourists.

L Tourists commit crimes and cause trouble in the bars and nightclubs.

M We have a beautiful country and we are proud that people want to visit us and find out more about us.

N Everyone is better off through tourism because all businesses get extra customers – ice-cream sellers, taxi drivers, market-stall holders – everyone.

O Local people cannot enjoy the tourist facilities because they are too expensive.

P Many local people can now buy cars, furniture and all sorts of things they could not afford before the tourists came.

Activity

In pairs, look at these opinions (A–P) from people who live in tourist destinations.

1 Draw a chart like the one below and sort the opinions into two lists:

Benefits of tourism	Problems of tourism

2 When you have done this, decide which views in each list you agree with and which ones you disagree with.
3 In what ways might some of the problems be reduced? Think about:
   a) what tourists could do.
   b) what the governments of the countries could do.
4 On balance, do you think tourism is good for a country?

6.5 How would you develop tourism in Myssia?

Imagine a small country on the edge of the Pacific Ocean. Call it Myssia. It is beautiful and undeveloped. It is a remote place, jutting out from the main land mass. On one side is the ocean and on the other high mountains which cut it off from other countries. Between the mountains and the ocean is a large, mainly flat plain. There is no airport and it can take three days to travel to the nearest big port in the neighbouring country. Myssia has one small port and a harbour, Igat, where ships call to bring visitors and people who want to do business with the inhabitants, the Myssi.

Only a few thousand people live in this small country. They live in huts and small houses containing little furniture. They have few possessions and do not use money a great deal, often bartering goods with each other. They mostly earn their living in three ways:

* farming – most of the farmers are pastoralists who graze their animals on the plains. But there is not a lot of water on the plains (it comes down from the mountains). The grassland is not rich, so they have to move their herds about quite a bit. A few farmers grow just enough crops and vegetables to support the rest of the population
* fishing
* diving for pearls from the reefs 3 km from shore.

The main trade goods are pearls, but a number of the inhabitants also make craft goods such as baskets and wood and stone carvings. They trade these goods with outsiders who come in a boat once a month bringing steel and iron goods such as knives and cooking utensils (there are no metal deposits in Myssia).

The land is very beautiful. There are long empty beaches lapped by crystal clear water. Great shoals of colourful tropical fish live around the reef. In the mountains, where few people live, there are rare birds and animals that have disappeared in other parts of the mainland. Myssia also has an ancient culture. There are stone circles and huge sculptures of figures all over the country that are not found anywhere else in the world. Religion is very strong and there are temples and shrines.

The one big drawback in Myssia is that there is not enough economic activity to keep young people there. Each year many leave to search for work in the big cities in the countries nearby. Those who return, usually only for visits, talk about all the things people have in these other countries: material possessions, television, pop music. Some of the Myssi would like to have similar things themselves, as well as developing their education and health services.

Read the description of Myssia. Work in small groups and use ideas from pages 122–125 to do this activity.

1 What aspects of Myssia would a tour operator like to exploit? These could include things to see and do, trips, and so on. What would you put in a holiday resort here to attract visitors?

2 Design an advert (for a colour magazine) tempting tourists to Myssia if the things you have suggested were developed there.

Developing Myssia

The potential for developing tourism in Myssia is enormous. There is space for buildings along the coast, and on the plains for an airport that could handle large jets. A number of foreign developers and tour operators wish to invest in the country. They want to build a large hotel complex and an airport. But before any plans can go ahead, they need permission from the government of Myssia. It is a democratic government that wants to put it to the people. Since Myssia has a small population, it is practical to consult everyone. The government has arranged a meeting of some of the main groups that are interested.

Work in groups of four or five. Each group should take on a different role. The roles are:

* foreign tour operators
* government of Myssia
* local farmers, fishermen and pearl divers
* religious leaders
* parents of young children and teenagers
* unemployed people
* the elderly (much respected in Myssia)
* international environmentalists, e.g. Greenpeace.

Before the meeting

Read your role brief (see pages 129–30) and, in your group, develop your arguments either *for* or *against* building an airport and a large hotel complex. Other developments, such as restaurants and shops, are likely to follow shortly afterwards if these two main ones go ahead.

* Think about how tourism would affect your group. Add any other points you can think of to the role brief.
* Talk about your group's position on tourism for Myssia and decide what arguments you will use in the meeting.
* Think about questions or demands you want to put to the foreign tour operators or to the government.
* Elect a spokesperson to put forward your point of view, although everyone will be able to speak at the meeting.

At the meeting

The government and the tour operators will sit at the front facing the audience. All other groups will sit in the audience. One member of the government (the Minister for Home Affairs) will chair the meeting (see page 38 for rules of meetings). The tour operators should present their case first in no more than five minutes. Then people in the audience can make points and ask questions. They should raise their hands to speak and wait to be called by the chairperson.

Vote

When everyone has had their say, the audience should vote on whether to agree to the development of tourism on Myssia.

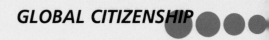
ROLE BRIEFS

Foreign tour operators

You can see great benefits to your companies from tourism in Myssia. Lots of tourists want to holiday off the beaten track, and you could make a lot of money. You will need to stress:

◆ the benefits of the deal to the government and people
◆ the extra money for the people who will work for you
◆ the jobs that will come to the country, not only in the airport and tourist complex but also in shops and restaurants and in supplying the hotels with food, etc.
◆ that you might agree to contribute a large sum of money for a new hospital, which is needed.

Prepare a presentation for the meeting. Tell the people how you would develop the tourist resort and the benefits for them. You could draft plans and a drawing of the buildings.

Government of Myssia

Your country is desperate for income. There are many poor people and young people are leaving, but many do not have the education to get good jobs elsewhere. From the tour operators at the meeting you want guarantees:

◆ that there will be enough jobs to keep everyone employed
◆ that the jobs will go to local people
◆ that the tour operators will pay towards education and training so that people can get skilled jobs in the tourist trade
◆ that Myssia will not be spoiled by hoards of tourists coming every year.

Religious leaders

The people of Myssia are deeply religious and have a strict moral code of behaviour. Young men and women do not spend time together alone before they are married and they cover their bodies at all times. You have heard about tourists and are worried that:

◆ your young people will learn bad habits
◆ tourists will uncover their bodies and dress in ways that are offensive to your religion
◆ tourists will not treat the temples and statues with respect
◆ the people of Myssia will become more interested in material goods and things like cars and pop music, and will turn away from the simple life that is the basis of your beliefs.

Local farmers, fishermen and pearl divers

At the moment, you can just about make ends meet from farming, fishing and diving for pearls. But fish stocks have suffered recently from a strange disease and the world price of pearls has fallen. If tourism comes to Myssia the fishermen and pearl divers are worried that:

◆ the fish might be badly affected by watersports and scuba divers
◆ your old houses along the quayside will be knocked down to build shops and restaurants.

The farmers are worried that:

◆ their land might be taken from them
◆ the hotels might use all the scarce water.

On the other hand, you will probably all be able to:

◆ sell your produce – pearls, fish, meat and vegetables – to hotels and restaurants and to tourists
◆ hire out your boats for fishing and diving, trips, etc.

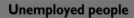

Unemployed people

You have not been able to get work in fishing and your family is too poor to support you on its small plot of land. You would like to leave the country to get a job on the mainland. However, you have a very basic education and you speak only Myssese. If tourism came to Myssia your concerns are:

◆ what jobs will be available?
◆ will you get one? You have heard that in other places, outsiders have been brought in to do the best jobs because they have the skills and experience
◆ will the tour operators provide training to teach you these skills?
◆ will the government help you to set up businesses, e.g. selling craft goods to tourists?

Elders

You have lived all your life in Myssia and love it. You love the quiet, the beauty and the friendliness of the people. You do not want your country to change, although you know that things will be different for your grandchildren. You have mixed feelings:

◆ you do not want your country's beauty to be spoiled
◆ you do not want to see your religious traditions lost.

But you are very poor so:

◆ you would like to feel that there will be money in the family to look after you in your old age
◆ you would like your young relations to be able to earn a living without having to leave the country.

Parents of young children and teenagers

You are worried about the future and how your children will be able to survive. Most of you are the families of farmers and fishermen. There is not enough work for everyone. You have mixed feelings about tourism:

◆ tourism might provide jobs
◆ tourist taxes might help the government build more schools
◆ you are worried about the likely increase in crime which you have been told often accompanies tourism
◆ you have relatives abroad who have told you about the ways tourists sometimes behave.

International environmentalists

Myssia is home to many rare and endangered species. You are certain that tourism will threaten the animal and plant life on land and in the ocean. The airport site would certainly destroy habitats. You also believe that holiday developments have spoiled the natural beauty of many parts of the world. You think the government should oppose the tour companies or limit the damage by putting strict restrictions on the tourist development. At the meeting you want to stress:

◆ the threat to wildlife
◆ the threat to the culture of the country, its religion and the traditional ways of doing things
◆ the way that when tourism arrives some people earn lots of money while others do not, and this tends to cause arguments and splits in society.

6.6 Tourism – the good, the bad and the ugly

Tourism can bring benefits to a whole country or to a particular region. Some parts of the UK rely on the tourist trade to bring money into their communities. The livelihoods of many people depend on tourism. But tourism can also have a bad impact on a country and the lives of the people who live there.

Activity

Make a copy of the chart below and make notes in the columns as you read through the three case studies.

What problems can tourism create?	What benefits can tourism bring?

CASE STUDY 1: LANGKAWI ISLAND IN MALAYSIA

Langkawi, with its sandy beaches and palm trees, is advertised to Europeans as a tropical paradise. Luxury hotels have sprung up and the airport is being extended. A new jetty has been built for passenger ferries and local fishermen were ordered to move their boats elsewhere. The shops and homes of people living near the jetty were demolished and replaced by a tourist shop and restaurant.

The people were paid well below the market rate for their property. The price of land on the island is soaring, so the islanders often end up in poor-quality housing on the least productive land.

The development of one luxury resort involved felling hundreds of coconut trees, filling in mangrove swamps and taking sand from the beaches, which is making the crystal clear water murky. Most of

the local people are angry because they feel their environment, culture and livelihoods are being sacrificed for the sake of tourist money. And they receive little of it! The hotels are owned and used by outsiders and most of the money from tourism goes to richer Malays or to foreigners.

CASE STUDY 2: HUNZA

Hidden away in the remote regions of Pakistan, high in the mountains, lies the land of Hunza. It is a small area less than 100 km long. It has a beautiful landscape of terraced fields, dry stone walls and poplar trees set amidst towering mountain peaks. Villages perch on rocky outcrops; the flat roofs of the stone houses are covered with drying corn and apricots. The Hunzakats are famed for their simple life and for living to a great age.

Until recently Hunza was virtually cut off from the world because it was so difficult to get to. In the nineteenth century bandits and warriors occupying hilltop forts operated in this lawless part of the northwest frontier. Then in 1978 the building of the Karakoram Highway changed that. The road brought the modern world to Hunza: education, transport, health, trade — and tourism. The Hunzakats were worried about the impact of this on their traditional way of life. So a Town

Management Society was set up to oversee the changes. They started projects to encourage traditional crafts and skills: woodcarving, building using traditional materials, weaving rugs of yakhair, an agricultural museum. The biggest project was the restoration of Baltit Fort above the capital of Karimabad. Until 1945 this was the residence of the rulers of Hunza. The restoration work gave jobs to local people who learned building and administration skills which were then used on restoring the stone houses around the fort. Sanitation, supplies of fresh water and electricity were brought in, encouraging people to return to the town.

Tourism played an important role in this. Tourists supplied the money that helped the local people to preserve their own heritage. There was even a revival of traditional festivals, such as the spring-blossom festival. The money from tourism and other projects went into the pockets of

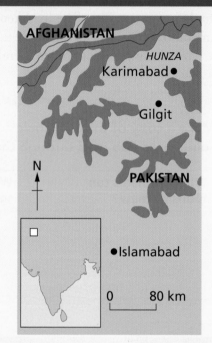

the local people. There was help from outside but foreign developers were not allowed to take over. The area has retained its natural beauty and its traditional culture which attract tourists who do not want to see it spoilt.

Tourists pay to visit Baltit Fort, which was restored by local people.

CASE STUDY 3: TANZANIA

The Maasai people live in the Serengeti area of Tanzania. They are pastoralists who graze cattle as a way of life. They believe that God made them the guardians of the cattle, which provide them with food, utensils, clothing and medicine. They believe that the land belongs to everybody.

In 1959 the Maasai were banned from taking their cattle into the western Serengeti, an area of great religious and cultural importance to them where warriors held ceremonies before going out to hunt lions and drew rock paintings. It was turned into a national park for tourists and now a luxury hotel has been built near the rock paintings and the Maasai cannot go there.

Another important area to the Maasai is the Ngorongoro Crater (made by an old volcano) which has water throughout the year and a salt lick, both essential to the

RWANDA
BURUNDI
ZAIRE
ZAMBIA
Serengeti National Park
Ngorongoro Crater
TANZANIA
MALAWI
MOZAMBIQUE
N
0   500 km

health of the cattle. However, the crater is also the most popular tourist attraction in Tanzania because of its vegetation and the hundreds of animal species living there.

On the rim of the crater there are now hotels and lodges for tourists who come on wildlife safari holidays run by foreign tour operators. The tourists compete with the Maasai for the scarce water in the crater

Tourism has had a bad effect on the Maasai people.

(tourists want showers and fresh water supplies). The Maasai are worried that they will be stopped from taking their cattle into the crater in the dry season, which coincides with the peak tourist season, because their cattle raise a lot of dust and drink the water.

These changes have had a bad effect on the Maasai culture and traditional way of life. The reduction and deterioration of the pasture land (because they are not allowed to move around so much) has affected the health of the cattle. Many families cannot now live by their livestock alone and face acute poverty. Young Maasai men and women line the main road hoping to earn money from tourists by selling craft goods and posing for pictures. They often earn more money than the elders do living the traditional way, and this is causing splits in Maasai society.

The Maasai have got little out of the tourist explosion. They are still waiting for improved water supplies and veterinary services. There are only four primary schools in the region and they are too far away for most children to attend. Tourism is contributing to the breakdown of their traditional way of life but brings the Maasai few benefits.

Activity

1 **What do you think are the main lessons to be learned from these case studies?**
2 **Do you think tourism should be stopped in some parts of the world?**
3 **Draw up a ten-point charter for the development of tourism, which would help to reduce the harmful effects it can have on the environment and people's lives.**

Tourists' Charter

* Tourists must respect the local people's lifestyles.

* Tourists must not harm the environment.

6.7 The United Kingdom and the European Union

The UK is geographically part of the continent of Europe. Because we are near to other European countries, we are more likely to travel to mainland Europe than to other countries in the world for holidays and work. We also have a long history of trade with other European countries. Despite past wars and disagreements, the countries of Europe depend on each other, particularly for trade.

European countries, particularly France, Italy and Germany, were anxious to get on well after the Second World War. In 1957, six countries signed the Treaty of Rome which brought the European Economic Community (EEC) into being. The aims of this were to encourage European countries to be friendly and not to fight wars again, but also to increase trade between them so that they could become more prosperous. The UK joined in 1973 because it could see the advantages of being part of a large trade bloc and did not want to be left out. By 1993 several more countries had joined and the EEC changed its name to the European Union (EU). (See Info page 138 for more about the EU.)

See Info page 138 for more about the EU.

Activity

1 **On an outline map of Europe, colour in the countries that belong to the European Union. Use the map on page 135 to help you.**
2 **On the same copy of the map, write the letter of each flag on the country to which it belongs.**
3 **Which other countries do you think might want to join the European Union? Why? Use the diagram below, showing the advantages of the EU, to help you to do this.**

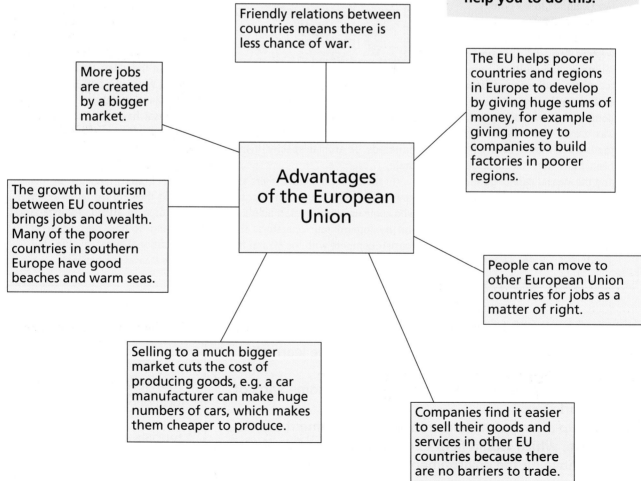

Friendly relations between countries means there is less chance of war.

More jobs are created by a bigger market.

The EU helps poorer countries and regions in Europe to develop by giving huge sums of money, for example giving money to companies to build factories in poorer regions.

The growth in tourism between EU countries brings jobs and wealth. Many of the poorer countries in southern Europe have good beaches and warm seas.

Advantages of the European Union

People can move to other European Union countries for jobs as a matter of right.

Selling to a much bigger market cuts the cost of producing goods, e.g. a car manufacturer can make huge numbers of cars, which makes them cheaper to produce.

Companies find it easier to sell their goods and services in other EU countries because there are no barriers to trade.

Member countries

Austria	Denmark	France	Greece	Italy
Finland	Luxembourg	Germany	Republic of Ireland	United Kingdom
Belgium	Portugal	Sweden	Spain	Netherlands

A B C D E F G H

I J K L M N O

How does the EU affect us?

Since the UK joined the EU, we have been able to travel freely to live and work in the countries of Europe and to sell our goods and services to these countries, without additional taxes or restrictions. But people still disagree about how far the affairs of this country should be decided by other member countries. The EU has rules about membership. All members have to agree to certain things, so that one country does not have an unfair trading advantage over another. These rules cause a lot of debate and disagreement.

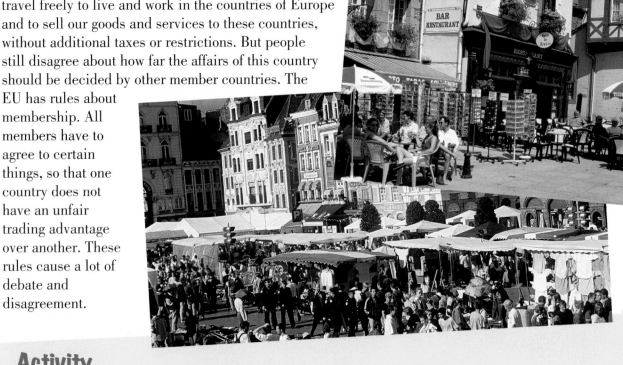

Activity

Work in pairs. Look at the headlines and news extracts below and at the top of the opposite page. Each one illustrates a different issue in our relationship with the European Union. For each one:

a) **decide what the issue is**
b) **explain why some people in Britain might be angry about it**
c) **give your view on the issue.**

WOULD CHOCOLATE BY ANY OTHER NAME TASTE AS SWEET?

WHAT IS CHOCOLATE? If you thought you knew, you obviously didn't know about cocoa solids. Sorry, but cocoa solids have to be a certain percentage of the mix, or it just ain't chocolate, according to a European directive. They say that British chocolate is not really chocolate because it does not use enough cocoa solids. British chocolate producers are protesting.

HOLIDAY WITH PAY, THANKS TO BRUSSELS

EVERYONE, part-time workers included, has a right to paid holiday from their job, thanks to a European Union ruling. Full-time workers get four weeks a year, part-timers get holiday according to how much they work. Unpaid leave to look after young children or dependants is also a right, again thanks to Europe. British businessmen say that these extra costs will make British companies uncompetitive in world trade and will lead to job losses.

IT'S KILOS FROM NOW ON

You can't buy a pound of tomatoes. It's going to have to be half a kilo, says the European Union. Will miles go next? How many kilometres in a mile? Ask your son or daughter if you don't know. They learn it in school.

FISH STOCKS MUST BE PROTECTED

Countries of the European Union are worried about low fish stocks. Fish are being taken out of the sea quicker than they can breed and replace themselves. Some fish are in danger of becoming extinct. The European Union has agreed to quotas for each country. This means that each fishing vessel is allowed to catch only a certain amount of each restricted species of fish. The rest must be thrown back. Fishermen in Cornwall and Scotland say they are being put out of business by the quotas.

Discuss

1 What do you think about Britain having to follow all the rules and regulations from Europe? (You can find out who makes these rules by looking at the organisations of the EU on Info page 138.)
2 Do you think the advantages of the EU (see page 134) mean that it's worth following the rules?
3 Do you care about the British pound or are you just as happy to have euro in your pocket?
4 Do you think it's a good idea that people can travel freely within Europe, to live and work in other countries in the EU?
5 Which of these two statements do you agree with?

A Britain has always been an independent island. We don't like being told what to do by other European countries. We want our Parliament to make all our laws. We like using pounds, which have our Queen's head on them, rather than euro. We like pounds and ounces, not kilos, and miles not kilometres.

B It's good to be closer to other European countries. Most of our trade is with them and we go on holiday there. We might as well have the same currency and weights. Working with our neighbours means that we will become better off. The rules are only there to make sure it is fair for all countries.

6 Debate in class whether you think Britain should get more or less involved in Europe. You can research this on the internet and find the arguments for and against.

The euro

At the beginning of 2002, the euro – a single European currency – was introduced in all the EU countries except Britain, Sweden and Denmark. On 1 January, these countries switched all their currencies to euro. This means that you can spend the same money in each of these countries and compare the prices of different goods.

6.8 European Union

In 1957 the European Economic Community (EEC), or Common Market, was created by the Treaty of Rome. Six countries signed the treaty. Its main aim was to create an economic union which would make it easier for the countries involved to trade with each other by removing all barriers to trade. It also aimed to unite the countries politically, after the terrible destruction of the Second World War, so that there could never be a major war between European countries again. Encouraging unity between the countries is seen by many as the most important reason for the EU.

Britain joined the EEC in 1973 along with several other countries. There have been some major developments in the organisation of the union, particularly in 1987 when the Single European Act was agreed by members and in 1993 when the Maastricht Treaty was signed, which bound member countries even closer together with a tighter set of rules. It was after this that the name European Union was adopted.

The main advantages of the European Union are seen as:

* a huge market of nearly 400,000 million people in which companies are able to sell their goods and services without restrictions because the economic barriers between countries have been removed
* citizens of the member states are able to move to and get jobs in the other member countries without restrictions
* EU citizens have a wide choice of goods and services, which are often cheaper because of competitive markets
* companies can produce goods more cheaply because they have a larger market for the same product.

Against this, some people in the member countries think:

* the European Union organisations have too much power and have taken away the right of the individual countries to make their own decisions about economic and other matters
* the EU is undemocratic, because decisions are taken a long way away from the people; people who are affected by the decisions have little chance to protest
* there are too many rules and regulations, some of which are not sensible
* a lot of money is wasted by the EU.

The main organisations of the European Union

* *The Commission* – Commissioners are chosen by the member countries to carry out the day-to-day work of the EU and to draft the policies (courses of action) they hope to follow.
* *The Council of Ministers* – each member state sends one minister. They discuss the policies that the Commissioners are proposing and agree or disagree with them. If they disagree then the proposals may be changed or abandoned.
* *The European Parliament* – Members of the European Parliament (MEPs) are elected in all the member countries. They meet together and debate the policies of the EU. Their discussions can result in things being changed or new ideas being put into practice.
* *The European Court of Justice* – this court settles disputes between member countries and also gives rulings on European law.

The headquarters of the EU (where the Commission is) is in Brussels.

The European Parliament meets in Strasbourg.

●●● Key words

authoritarian enforcing strict control; obedience to authority as opposed to individual freedom

campaign the activities that candidates and their supporters undertake to persuade people to vote for them

censorship banning or changing material (newspaper articles, books, films, photographs) to prevent it being seen by the public

child labour children under the age of fifteen who work to help support their families or themselves

civil liberties the right to freedom of speech and action

collective responsibility a whole group taking responsibility for the decisions its members make or the actions they take

community involvement taking an active part in the local community

constituency the voters in a particular area who elect an MP to parliament

Council Tax money paid to the council by residents of an area to pay for local services

court a place where a judge or magistrate tries cases and sentences those found guilty

democracy a system of government where people regularly elect their leaders and have a say in the way a country is governed

discrimination treating someone unfairly as a result of prejudice

election a way of choosing someone for a particular position by voting

environmental impact the effect that something has on the environment

equal opportunities getting a fair chance, regardless of gender, race, religion or other beliefs, to receive an education, get a job and promotion, obtain housing, etc.

fact something that can be proved to be true

fair trade paying farmers in the developing world a fair price for the goods they produce

human rights rights that are held to belong to any person. The United Nations Universal Declaration of Human Rights, 1948, sets out a full list of the rights that all people should have.

These include the rights to life, liberty, education, freedom of movement and equality before the law.

justice the administration of the law according to accepted principles

law a rule that has the backing of the government

legal system the processes and institutions that make and uphold our laws

magistrate a member of the local community who deals with cases that are brought before magistrates' and youth courts

manifesto a statement of policies and aims

motion a proposal put to a meeting

news values the characteristics of a news story that will make people want to read or listen

offender someone who has broken the law

opinion what someone thinks about a particular issue; not a fact

Parliament the place where people meet to discuss important issues, make laws and question the government about the way it is running the country

police the people who enforce the law and maintain order and public safety

political party an organised group of people who have a particular set of values

press freedom the ability of the press to write what they like

pressure group an organisation that has strong opinions on a particular issue and attempts to influence the people who make decisions

propaganda information presented in such a way that it assists the cause of a government or group

protest a public show of disagreement

sentence the punishment given to a person who has been found guilty in a court

services jobs done by the local council for the benefit of people living in the area it controls, e.g. running the local library, collecting rubbish, cleaning the streets

tourism travelling to other countries to enjoy holidays, usually sightseeing

Index